"CCA has helped us 'up' our own high expectations of ourselves. We have streamlined our sales process and provided our team with new tools and techniques, our marketing is more effective and ROI-focused than ever, and our implementation process is tight and run by a cross-functional team. The best part is that I have more energy, focus, and time than ever before. Our new incentive plans, accountability structure, executive team code of conduct, ranking of high- and low-value activities, and other techniques have provided the executive team members with five to ten hours of strategic time per person each week. I knew we had a great team, and I see now that they're capable of far more than I could've dreamed. Thanks, CCA!"

—JASON BEANS, CEO, Rising Medical Solutions

"When I first met Christine I wasn't sure what the return on investment in coaching could truly be. Now I know what it is: I think bigger working with Christine—we will double (or greater) our revenue this year as a result of my increased ability to create new strategies, expand my vision, see into my blind spots. She helped me create accountability structures and communication rhythms so everyone is aligned and charging forward. In less than 120 days we closed the largest deal in our company's history using the strategy Christine and I created together. I know what's going to happen next—we'll exceed our sales quota. Again. This is now how we roll. Thanks, CCA! Thanks, Christine!"

—SHARON MACDONALD, CEO, Interim Furnishings

"The results have been terrific. In our first six months working together, Christine helped me delegate low-value activities and gain fifteen hours of strategic time per week, optimize our sales pipeline and process, get me out of stress and into peace and increased performance, and streamline both marketing and account management. Christine is personable, creative, extremely intuitive, and understands the steps needed for a company to consistently grow. I highly recommend CCA for any organization that wants to take their company to the next level and build a great team."

—GAIL TOLSTOI-MILLER, CEO, Consultnetworx

"I've been in boardrooms around the world, and I've been in the C-suite for many years. I thought I'd learned a great deal about leadership and culture in my roles as COO and CFO at Patagonia, and CEO at Smith & Hawken. Then I met Christine. Our team has come together in a way I couldn't have imagined prior to coaching with CCA. We now have the right people in the right roles with the right tools on the right initiatives. Our revenue and profitability is rapidly growing; our culture is rich, honest, and thriving; and our team is rising up and performing at unparalleled levels. I always knew we had this in us! Thanks for helping us to help ourselves, CCA."

—KARYN BARSA, CEO, Coyuchi

"Christine has been very effective in helping me establish a strong meeting and communication rhythm, which has increased our team's morale and improved our culture. She has provided practical advice on rewards/consequences and increasing our alignment. We have implemented systems to improve our accountability, which has led to our largest pipeline in history and more proactive sales activity across the firm. I am really excited about where we are going and greatly appreciate all that Christine is doing for us."

—SCOTT EISENBERG, Managing Partner, Amherst Partners, LLC

"Working with CCA has made a huge positive difference for us in sales, marketing, culture, operational efficiency, and leadership overall. Our sales plan is now streamlined, and our reps have compelling new incentives. We've put in place a solid ROI structure and can cost-justify our marketing. As a result of our work with CCA I have increased visibility of each department and can help guide our company more effectively. Operational efficiency at our company has reached a new level—and we're raising the bar. The best part is that our culture is deepening, our team is emotionally engaged, and we know where we're going and how to get there."

—ASHA CHAUDHARY, CEO, Jaipur Rugs

"CCA has helped me to become a more effective leader in the eyes of my team members, my colleagues, my strategic partners, and the loved ones in my personal life. Our team loves working with Christine. They are now more aligned, are closely tracking to our goals, and are more emotionally engaged and accountable. We've recently had the two best months of our history, and the trend continues upward. We're on track to significantly increase revenue and profitability in the coming year. CCA has truly 'moved the needle' for our business."

—DIONE SPITERI, CEO, U.S. Appraisal Group

"If you want to gain tremendous clarity on your business strategy and priorities, consider CCA. CCA's best value comes in changing mindsets and improving strategies in an environment that is ready to rapidly grow. If you're a CEO or executive on a rapid growth trajectory, and you want to be the best leader possible for your team, with CCA you'll experience unparalleled levels of insight, growth, and support. We're highly profitable and are diversifying into new markets, revenues continue to exceed our projections, and our team is deeply coming together. Thanks, CCA!"

—SABETAY PALATCHI, CEO, General Financial

"I'd heard about executive coaching for a while, yet was fairly skeptical regarding the return on investment. Within the first six months my leadership style evolved in ways I couldn't have imagined. Using the tools I've gained from CCA, especially the neuroscience rapport techniques, I now more quickly and deeply connect with our team, clients, and prospects. The inquiry techniques have enabled me to more rapidly create a culture of leadership at all levels, helping our team to take greater ownership faster. Our profit is soaring and our people are performing at record levels. Thanks, CCA, for helping us to grow into who we'd always hoped to be."

—MARK PAYNE, President, ReliaMax Surety Group

"Before working with CCA we weren't always working effectively as a team. Within one day of CCA's training, we had over 33% of our *entire* company ask for more responsibility and to have the bar raised on their leadership contribution. As a result of our work with CCA, our morale is higher. Our retention is up. We've had record levels of revenue for several months and we're seeing real gains in cross-functional team productivity. Our CEO now calls Talent the Heart and Soul of the organization."

—RICK THOMPSON,
VP Talent Management and Administration, Rising Medical Solutions

"We're a high-performance service team in a very complex business with very demanding customers. We've been 'hard at it' tasked with delivering huge savings and other value contributions to the business year after year. We also reduced our head count significantly during the same time. Christine Comaford spent time with our team talking about how we could use her learnings to reenergize, beat bureaucracy, and put excitement back into the job. We're a tough group . . . but it was transformational. She's the best!"

—GREGG BRANDYBERRY, Former Vice President,
Procurement, Global Systems and Operations, GlaxoSmithKline

"How do you inspire a global sales force to adopt new, high-velocity sales techniques and get beyond 'no' even in the face of a down economy? Christine Comaford. That's how. Thanks for rocking our sales conference! Your proven tactics for sales and life success left everyone inspired, invigorated, and ready to exceed their quotas!"

—TIM MINAHAN, CMO, Ariba, Inc.

"When the Oval Office says 'jump!,' the only question is, 'how high?' Christine helped us develop and launch our intranet strategy, which was super-aggressive for standard-pace government workers. She got everyone past the fear of change and into the excitement of it—and now Americans have access to far more government data via self-serve websites. Christine's contribution to creating a government that works better and costs less was critical."

—GREG WOODS, National Performance Review, Clinton administration

"When my boss said he wanted me to increase our top line sales by 30% *fast* I was wondering how I'd do it. We're a huge company, and growth like this doesn't happen overnight. CCA helped us to use the latest neuroscience techniques to shift the state of our sales team to a more positive and empowered state, to streamline our sales process, to develop rapid rapport with our prospects and partners, to more deeply engage with our sales and service teams. The result is that we now have *massive momentum*. . . . we have a clear and rapid path to our increased sales, we're getting more meetings, we're closing faster, we're having a lot more fun and less stress. I have new tools to develop my sales team faster and keep them on track. Thanks, CCA, for helping us sell at the level I always knew we could."

—TOM MOORE, Director of Sales and Marketing, Baxter Manufacturing

"Our members rely on us to provide them with leading-edge speakers and breakthrough ideas. Christine keynoted our annual CEO conference and got a standing ovation. Need I say more? Nope."

—MIKE SANSOLO, Senior Vice President, Food Marketing Institute

"Our client appreciation event was our best ever—thanks to you, Christine! You reinforced our brand as the financial adviser whose finger is on the pulse of what the high-net-worth individual needs. Our clients and prospects were enthralled, entertained, and eager to take decisive action regarding their financial future."

—JOY BOATWRIGHT, Senior Financial Advisor, Merrill Lynch Global Private Client Services

"Christine's coaching has been instrumental in accelerating growth in my company from 2011 to 2012—triple digit this last year. She pushes, she paws at existing structures, and she insists on performance. Great investment!" —LISA CALHOUN, CEO, Write2Market; 2012 Female Entrepreneure of the Year Finalist, American Business Awards; Atlanta Top 23 Entrepreneur, 2012; Past President, EO Atlanta

"Christine delivered a thought-provoking keynote at our recent client and team appreciation event. The audience was entertained, encouraged, and gently challenged to take their careers and lives to the next level. Christine's pragmatic techniques for reinventing oneself, increasing connection with others, and delivering results were all spot-on. The feedback has been phenomenal!"

—KIM HOPKINS, SR. Vice President, Area Sales Manager, Business Banking, National City Bank

"Your keynote at our client appreciation event was a smashing success! Thanks for a lively, inspirational, thought-provoking program. I know everyone left with tangible takeaways to both excel in their careers and lead balanced, fulfilling lives. Thanks, Christine!"

—KYLEEN FISHWICK, Integrated Account Manager, Businessweek

"If you need a speaker to engage your most difficult audience—'Type A,' dynamic business leaders who are often difficult to engage—you need Christine Comaford. Her ideas and techniques are both specific and actionable when it comes to generating predictable revenue, building passionate teams, and driving profitable growth, and are delivered in a fun and fascinating way. Our clients are still talking about her presentation and consider it our best yet! Put her in front of your toughest audience and you won't be disappointed!"

—SUNNY NUNAN, President & Founder, Core24

"For the past eighteen years, I have hired hundreds of speakers. Over the years, one speaker's message runs into the next and the thrill of hearing speakers' presentations and messages has dulled. Yet when I read Christine Comaford's book *Rules for Renegades*, I knew she was different and that I had to hire her and bring her to my YPO client, Global One. Christine speaks from her heart and her personal experience with a lot of value to business owners. She shares real information for a real person facing real challenges in their business and her accountable coaching strategy for executives gets measurably improved results and a positive impact on corporate profits. I highly recommend Christine. My client YPO Global One rated her presentation a perfect 10!!!"

—SAMANTHA BORLAND, Chapter Administrator, YPO Global One Chapter

SMARTTRIBES

SMART
TRIBES

How Teams Become
Brilliant Together

Christine Comaford

Portfolio / Penguin

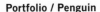

PORTFOLIO / PENGUIN
Published by the Penguin Group
Penguin Group (USA) Inc., 375 Hudson Street,
New York, New York 10014, USA

USA / Canada / UK / Ireland / Australia / New Zealand / India / South Africa / China

Penguin Books Ltd, Registered Offices: 80 Strand, London WC2R 0RL, England
For more information about the Penguin Group visit penguin.com

SmartTribes was first published by Morgan James Publishing. It has been revised and
expanded for this Portfolio / Penguin edition.

ISBN: 9781591846482

Printed in the United States of America
10 9 8 7 6 5 4 3 2 1

Book design by Elyse Strongin, Neuwirth & Associates, Inc.
Set in Janson Text LT Std.

To the remarkable leaders and members of the SmartTribes
I've had the great good fortune to work with in the past,
those I am working with in the present,
and those I will work with in the future.

You inspire me.

CONTENTS

[PART ONE]

Why Every Leader Needs a SmartTribe   7

FOREWORD

SmartTribes is dynamic, fast-paced, and full of insights that are incredibly valuable to executives who are looking to create positive and lasting cultural change in their organizations.

In this high-octane and insightful book, Christine Comaford gives us a systematic approach to creating what she calls a SmartTribe—a company culture that will outperform, outsell, and outinnovate the competition. Christine's approach is unique in that it is from the inside out. It helps us change our company's and culture's ecosystem and as such generates results for the long term.

Having been recently recognized as the #1 leadership thinker in the world by Thinkers50 (sponsored by the *Harvard Business Review*), I can say that I know a thing or two about leadership, behavioral change, and executive coaching, and Christine is spot-on in her discussion of emotional triggers! She calls them "emotional hijacks," those little interrupts throughout your day that remind you of a person, a relationship, a relative, a situation at work. These codes that were written into our psyches when we were very young play out in our adult life. They can keep successful people from being even more successful.

In fact, any human being will tend to repeat behavior that is followed by positive reinforcement. And the more successful we become, the more positive reinforcement we get, the more likely we are to experience the success delusion: I behave this way. I am successful. Therefore, I must be successful because I behave this way. Not so!

The method for change that Christine puts forth in *SmartTribes* will help you change your repeated behavior, especially when it no longer serves you, to that which will take you to the highest peaks of performing. Even better, it will help you as a leader assist your people to get the results they would like, too. Christine's goal is to help you increase your own and your team's performance, innovation, and engagement. And if you do as she suggests in the pages that follow, it will happen!

So, get ready to launch into a new dimension of performance. With Christine as your guide, you will be amazed with the results!

Life is good.

MARSHALL GOLDSMITH,

author of the *New York Times* best sellers *MOJO* and
What Got You Here Won't Get You There and #1 leadership thinker

SMARTTRIBES

INTRODUCTION

MY PROMISE:
THE ROI OF A SMARTTRIBE

L uke, the CEO of a thriving midwestern transportation company, was barely managing 63% growth per year. He couldn't hire people fast enough, his team was on the verge of burnout, he had twelve direct reports, and he worked all the time. His greatest concern was that he'd have a heart attack or lose his marriage before he reached the goal line: selling the company for $500 million.

Luke approached me after I spoke at a joint Stanford-MIT event where I outlined the process for optimizing teams in rapid growth and turnaround scenarios. After a brief interview the diagnosis was clear: he needed a SmartTribe. We applied the techniques in this book to his business and here's what happened: Luke maintained his growth pace; further cultivated the leadership team to help balance his workload; streamlined the executive team's focus, influence, and clarity; and ended the burnout. Today his company is worth $425 million. Next year he'll be ready to sell it for $500 million. His goal is now within reach, his team is happy and energized, and his marriage has never been better.

When leaders call me, they want three things from their teams (and often themselves): increased performance, increased innovation, and increased emotional engagement. They're heading toward the next level of revenue, and what worked in the past just isn't working anymore.

They're stymied.

They're stuck.

They aren't getting the results they want.

Sound familiar?

What you need isn't more tactical advice. What you need is a systematic approach that changes your company culture from the inside out and generates results all on its own. In this book, I'm going to teach you how to create a SmartTribe, a company culture that will consistently outperform, outsell, and outinnovate your competition.

Why "smart"? Because the proactive, innovative part of the brain is consistently in the driver's seat. In this state, we're able to access all of our internal resources and respond from choice instead of reacting impulsively from fear. We're able to envision an exciting future and feel drawn and compelled by it, as we eagerly anticipate the exciting rewards it holds.

Why "tribe"? There's a reason *tribe* has become the new buzzword; the latest neuroscience research shows that our very sense of survival depends upon a sense of belonging. When that sense of belonging isn't there, even in the workplace, fear kicks in. And our primal survival "fight/flight/freeze" brain takes the driver's seat and kicks our innovative brain to the curb. A tribe is all about collaboration, connection, shared goals, and emotional engagement. Our feeling of tribe is fostered by our company's culture, which we'll optimize in the coming chapters. And even if you're working alone, you have extended team members—whether they are contractors, service providers, or friendly sounding boards. Very few projects can be completed by one person working in a vacuum.

Yet as leaders we often unintentionally send our teams into the part of their brains where optimal performance is tremendously compromised. This can happen when a company

- Is navigating rapid growth where internal priorities are frequently shifting and the team is challenged to quickly adapt and stretch
- Has unclear directives
- Has inconsistent accountability structures and communication rhythms
- Has a culture where the blind spots and challenging behaviors of the leaders are not being addressed

- Has unresolved conflict and/or low alignment among the leadership of the company
- Is changing its business model or executing a complete company turnaround

All of the above are common in growth scenarios. And all of the above can put our teams into fight/flight/freeze, or what in this book we'll call the Critter State, without access to our greatest resources.

In contrast, the Smart State is where we have full access to creativity, problem solving, innovation, higher consciousness, and emotional engagement. We all want our companies to grow, and change is always a part of growth. So we all need to learn techniques to avoid sending our teams into their Critter State and to help them shift into—and stay in—their Smart State. If your entire culture is consistently operating in its Smart State, then you've got a SmartTribe. This is when our *team* becomes a true *tribe*.

So what does this SmartTribe culture look like? Even in the face of change and growth, SmartTribes are focused and communicate clearly and directly. They are unusually accountable to their promises and powerfully influential. And they have the energy and enthusiasm to do what needs to be done—consistently.

If you don't have a SmartTribe and want one, or you want to make your SmartTribe even smarter, this book will show you how you got where you are, how to get clear on where you want to go, and how to use potent neuroscience techniques to get there. These techniques are easy to learn, practical to use, and will ensure you and your team move forward, reach the next revenue inflection point, and do so with energy, engagement, and innovation.

They'll also give you the power to leave your competitors in the dust. Sound intriguing?

Here are some results from the SmartTribes we've helped create. Note that the ranges can be quite wide, based on the company size and the length of time the team has been operating as a SmartTribe.

- Sales closed up to 50% faster and close rate up by 44%+
- Revenues and profits increased up to 201% annually%
- Marketing demand generation increased up to 237%
- Individuals are up to 50% more productive and emotional engagement, loyalty, accountability increased up to 100%

- New products and services developed up to 48% faster.
- Marketing messages are up to 301% more effective.

Here are a few more results from individual team members in a SmartTribe:

- 97% tangibly contributed to increasing key executive strategic/high-value time by five to fifteen hours per week.
- 63% received a promotion to a role with increased responsibility and management of others within six months of applying our techniques via coaching and training.
- 100% increased their ability to significantly influence others and outcomes.
- 86% reported getting more done in less time due to the accountability techniques they learned.
- 100% reported the ability to apply our communication techniques and thinking styles both at home and at work, resulting in an increase in personal fulfillment.

Here's the bigger picture, thanks to Harvard Business School's eleven-year study on the impact of performance-enhancing cultures:

TABLE 0-1. IMPACT OF PERFORMANCE-ENHANCING CULTURES

	Average increase for twelve firms with performance-enhancing cultures	Average increase for twenty firms without performance-enhancing cultures
Revenue growth	682%	166%
Employment growth	282%	36%
Stock price growth	901%	74%
Net income growth	756%	1%

Source: James Heskett and John Kotter, *Corporate Culture and Performance* (Free Press, 1992), validated by clients of Christine Comaford Associates, LLC.[1]

This groundbreaking research in 1992 by Harvard Business School professor James Heskett detailed the corporate cultures of two hundred companies and how each company's culture affected its long-term economic performance. Heskett and John Kotter published a book, *Corporate Culture and Performance*, that explained the study and demonstrated the value of investing in culture. A lot has happened since this data was released; there have been countless discoveries in applying neuroscience techniques to increase leadership, emotional engagement, and performance even more profoundly. The key is having the tools and techniques to replicate the above results in your own culture. Hence this book.

Having a SmartTribe becomes essential if you want to:

- Navigate rapid growth where internal priorities are frequently shifting and the team is challenged to quickly adapt and stretch
- Increase accountability, communication, and execution among team members, resulting in profound revenue, profit, and market position growth
- Resolve conflict or improve alignment of business partners, teams, and board members
- Improve the leadership and communication skills of C- and VP-level executives by helping them overcome their blind spots and challenging behaviors, and expand their vision
- Execute a new business model or complete company turnaround with executive and cultural support

My combination of more than thirty years of operational experience plus more than thirty-five years of expertise in behavioral modification, human potential, and organizational change is the secret behind creating SmartTribes.

And now the secret is yours.

How to Get the Most from This Book

See this book as your field guide. I'm your scout. I have run ahead of you and I'm here waiting, machete in hand, to show you the most efficient and effective path. Did you see the movie *The King's Speech*? If so, think of me as Lionel, the speech therapist. Like Lionel, I am neither a medical doctor nor a neuroscientist. I'm a business builder in the trenches who applies a wide variety of techniques in order to generate meaningful real-world results.

Read the book from start to finish, or drill down on the chapters as you need them. Do the Assess, Act, and ROI exercises at the end of each chapter, apply the Resources, and you'll be amazed by your results. Try the templates and additional materials we've provided in the appendix to jump-start your SmartTribe. And come back to the book when you're stuck, stressed, or not getting the results you want. You can use it as a helpful refresher and reminder of some techniques you may not have used yet.

We all have stuck spots—those blind spots where we ache to move forward but somehow can't. What if you could see ahead, and either move through potential stuck spots or navigate around them? What if you could see into the stuck spots of your key team members and help them through or around these treacherous time and energy wasters? With this level of vision, you could also see where the market is going, and get there first—or at least arrive better prepared than your competition. That's one reason you're reading this book: to see the present more clearly and to intentionally create the future you want.

In this book, you'll get the tools to improve your vision, create a culture where you and your team can fully access your best resources, and improve performance constantly and naturally as your company grows. You'll get the tools to get and stay Smart.

Ready? Let's become brilliant together.

WHY EVERY LEADER NEEDS A SMARTTRIBE

1.

HOW GREAT COMPANIES GET STUCK

There's a war for talent out there. In the 2012 Pricewaterhouse-Coopers CEO Survey,[1] the consulting firm found that having (or not having) the right talent in place can impact innovation, market opportunities, the ability to deliver on strategic initiatives, growth, and quality of output. Talent was the number one concern for CEOs. Period. Look at how CEOs responded when asked "How have talent constraints impacted your company's growth and profitability over the past twelve months?" The results were telling; talent had a huge impact on their performance.

KEY ISSUE: How have talent constraints impacted your company's growth and profitability over the past 12 months?	USA CEO Results	Global CEO Results
Cancelled or delayed a key strategic initiative	22%	24%
Unable to pursue a market opportunity	24%	29%
Weren't able to innovate effectively	20%	31%
Couldn't achieve growth forecasts where they were based	16%	24%
Quality standards fell	16%	21%
Talent-related expenses rose more than expected	43%	43%

But there's only so much top talent out there, and your energy should not be—and cannot be—spent solely on replacing or recruiting talent. At the end of the day, you've got to maximize the talent that you have.

Leaders often assume their company's growth depends on finding and fixing problems. They want their salespeople to sell more, their engineers to innovate faster and with greater ingenuity, their client-care people to better service accounts, and on and on. And in the rare cases where increasing revenue isn't the priority, increasing profit is.

Hey, who wouldn't want to solve all these problems? Yet these are not the real problems. They are merely symptoms of underlying structural problems, indications of people getting stuck in their Critter State—in fight, flight, or freeze. And leaders often put their teams exactly there, albeit unintentionally.

When companies grow, they come to certain places where the things that used to work, the things that created a level of success, don't work anymore. We call these *inflection points*. And these crucial points are tied to revenue and company growth.

Are You Approaching an Inflection Point?

Here's the trouble with inflection points: at each one you have a whole new company. At each inflection point, a company must reinvent itself in

Figure 1-1. What Happens at Revenue Inflection Points

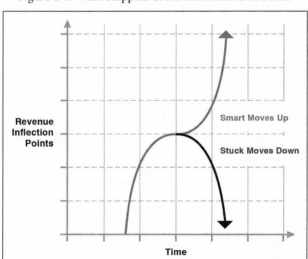

order to reach it and move through it. If a company doesn't adapt, it will become stuck and ultimately decline into a parabolic upside-down curve, rather than an undulation back into growth mode. (See figure 1-1.)

How do you navigate between inflection points? How do you maintain and increase your momentum to avoid organizational stuck spots—the spots of stasis usually found between inflection points where the company stops growing and swirls around at approximately the same level of annual revenue before sliding precipitously backward? How do you get into the Smart State—the safe, secure, intelligent state of teamwork that will get you to the next inflection point, when the game reaches the next level?

To reach that next inflection point, you will need to intentionally map out a plan to get there, and then execute that plan with determination. Either you keep doing what you're doing, barely maintaining the same revenue year after year, or you slide back down to the previous inflection point, or you move forward with tremendous intentionality. The world is full of "living dead" companies that reached an inflection point and couldn't grow to the next one. You're either moving forward or moving back. Stasis is not sustainable.

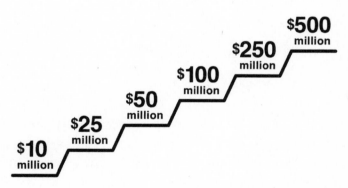

Figure 1-2. Some Common Revenue Inflection Points

In case you're about to dive into your Critter State, let me throw you a line. One thing that's reassuring about inflection points is that they are relatively predictable; we consistently see companies getting stuck at specific revenue levels. That's the good news; you'll be able to see that next inflection point in your future and know what you need to focus on: shifts in people (and culture), money (sales and financing), and business model (which includes marketing).

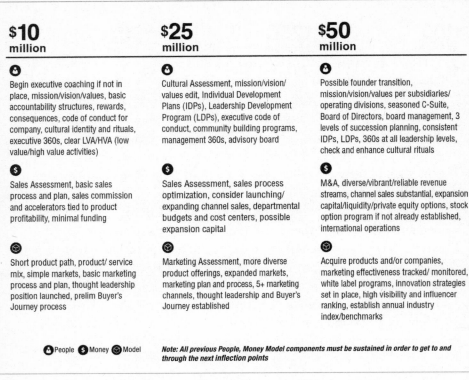

$10 million	$25 million	$50 million
👤	👤	👤
Begin executive coaching if not in place, mission/vision/values, basic accountability structures, rewards, consequences, code of conduct for company, cultural identity and rituals, executive 360s, clear LVA/HVA (low value/high value activities)	Cultural Assessment, mission/vision/values edit, Individual Development Plans (IDPs), Leadership Development Program (LDPs), executive code of conduct, community building programs, management 360s, advisory board	Possible founder transition, mission/vision/values per subsidiaries/operating divisions, seasoned C-Suite, Board of Directors, board management, 3 levels of succession planning, consistent IDPs, LDPs, 360s at all leadership levels, check and enhance cultural rituals
💲	💲	💲
Sales Assessment, basic sales process and plan, sales commission and accelerators tied to product profitability, minimal funding	Sales Assessment, sales process optimization, consider launching/expanding channel sales, departmental budgets and cost centers, possible expansion capital	M&A, diverse/vibrant/reliable revenue streams, channel sales substantial, expansion capital/liquidity/private equity options, stock option program if not already established, international operations
🔷	🔷	🔷
Short product path, product/ service mix, simple markets, basic marketing process and plan, thought leadership position launched, prelim Buyer's Journey process	Marketing Assessment, more diverse product offerings, expanded markets, marketing plan and process, 5+ marketing channels, thought leadership and Buyer's Journey established	Acquire products and/or companies, marketing effectiveness tracked/ monitored, white label programs, innovation strategies set in place, high visibility and influencer ranking, establish annual industry index/benchmarks

👤 People 💲 Money 🔷 Model   *Note: All previous People, Money Model components must be sustained in order to get to and through the next inflection points*

Figure 1-3a. How to Navigate Common Revenue Inflection Points

What Has to Change?

To continue to grow, to undulate upward at an inflection point, an organization needs to make changes in one or more of the following areas: people, money, and model. Here are some common inflection points and what to look for, so that you can determine how urgently you need to get to work.

People. Some of your team members may need to develop profound new skill sets, behaviors, capabilities, beliefs, or identities. Regardless, they'll likely need to become more emotionally engaged and have their lights turned up to shine brighter. As the organization passes the higher revenue inflection points, the CEO will need to step back more and more, empowering the executive team to take more responsibility, and in the extreme this can mean a large-scale organizational and/or cultural overhaul.

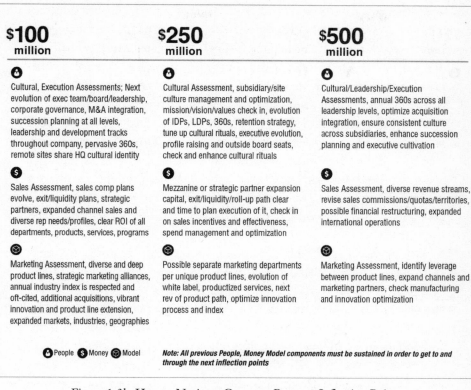

Figure 1-3b. How to Navigate Common Revenue Inflection Points

The only way to break the endless cycles of an organizational stuck spot is to start treating the system instead of individual symptoms. But here's the hitch: organizations (systems) tend to be reflections of all the people who work there—especially the leaders. And that means that in order for your organization to change, everyone has to be involved, starting at the very top and working all the way down the organizational chart to the people on the front lines. It also means leaders must work on themselves. This section of figures 1-3a and 1-3b shows you what people work to do to ensure you reach the inflection point.

Money. At each inflection point, you'll want to ask a number of money-related questions. How is the business funded? Do you need expansion capital? How are departmental budgets created (or not)? How are costs accounted for, and what is the discipline in reporting? Financial systems must be looked into and explicitly altered to fit the next inflection point.

How efficient are your operations? Have you streamlined all expenses? Do you track ROI on all projects—internal and external? How are your sales? What's the process of creating and converting new business? Are your incentive programs working? Are sales commissions tied to profit per sale? What are your sales channels? Both your top and bottom lines must be aligned with your growth goal.

To grow to the next inflection point, your systems must be aligned and your funding model must be appropriate. Don't forget strategic partners, industry influencers, and key alliances, as well as liquidity event planning. Outsourcing or sale of nonperforming or low-margin business lines needs to be considered here too. This section of figures 1-3a and 1-3b shows you what money work to do to ensure you reach the inflection point.

Model. Moving through inflection points also requires taking a close look at your business model. What does your business model look like now? How will the organization grow—organically or via acquisition? As an organization grows, core competencies shift, markets (customers, competitors, environment, distribution channels, and technology) evolve, and some opportunities are more leverageable than others. What is today's product line? Tomorrow's? How is your product path working and how can you scale your relationships with clients, strategic alliances, and key influencers? How effective is your marketing?

To grow to the next inflection point, you need a strategic plan. What is yours? Does it include growing through new products, fewer products, acquisitions, or consolidation of your industry or market sector? Do you need to spin off or outsource a nonperforming division? Does it make sense to shift your business model to streamline profit potential? This section of figures 1-3a and 1-3b shows you what business model work to do to ensure you reach the inflection point.

People Are the Toughest: An Inflection Point Example

Inflection points apply to any business—even divisions of businesses. A large publisher came to us with a challenge: their new magazine was rapidly approaching the $25 million inflection point and it was about to implode. Instead of rejoicing that they'd be profitable two years before projected, the leadership team was losing sleep and fearing the loss of key advertisers. Why? Their top sales and editorial team members were job hunting. Of course, it's easier to find a new gig when you're part of a hot new property. But why were they so eager to leave?

We quickly performed a Cultural Assessment and uncovered several challenges, all people-related. Employees below the VP level had no career path. Why stick around if management wasn't actively helping you to advance—even when you had repeatedly asked for more responsibility? Management sorely needed to increase transparency across the entire company and all of its divisions. People would get promoted and fired with little understanding as to why. It appeared many executives were professional brownnosers, and yet the people who truly delivered the bottom line results were overlooked at promotion time.

To fix this company's people problem and keep them moving healthily through the upcoming inflection point, we implemented several keys that got the company back on track—with a SmartTribe on board. We'll see them in further detail later in the book. Here's what happened. First, we put accountability structures in place to track performance for all to see. Next, we helped create Individual Development Plans (IDPs) to map out and track the evolution of each employee's career (more on this in our Leading from the Inside Out kit per the Resources below), rolled out executive coaching to senior management to help support these cultural changes, and announced a Leadership Development Program (LDP).

Throughout the process leadership stayed in constant communication with the team to increase transparency and alignment. Six months into the process, employee retention across the company is the highest it's ever been. And now that the people side is humming, they'll focus on money and model to reach their next inflection point.

In my thirty-plus years of helping clients build market-leading businesses, evolving and optimizing one's people—the company's culture—is always the hardest part of the process. This is because people are emotional, complex, remarkable beings with tremendous ranges in behavior, many of which are unpredictable. Without people, the money and model don't matter—because there isn't anyone around to make them happen! Money and model are also simpler because they're based on our intellect and empirical evidence, not on our emotions. So in this book we're going to spend our time together focusing on your people and on developing a SmartTribe to ensure we can navigate the above inflection points with great momentum and as much ease and fun as possible. Let's get started.

Get into High Gear: SmartTribe Accelerators

In the Industrial Revolution, scientific management principles emerged to cope with the need to produce more, better, faster. In the Information Age, some of these principles and practices are still sound—hey, let's not throw the baby out with the bathwater—but some feel as obsolete as the Ford Edsel they were designed to produce.

I have noticed that leaders who are able to grow their organizations rapidly in the face of accelerating technological and societal change—the people who create and foster innovation—exhibit certain characteristics. I call these characteristics **SmartTribe Accelerators**. And the leaders who use them are the ones who pull their companies to and through inflection points.

You see, people are essentially unmanageable. Most attempts to control and manipulate people will ultimately fail. Since we're dealing with an American workforce where 71% of workers are emotionally disengaged and simply working for the money,[2] we know it's essential to fix our state of so-called leadership.

"Old school" management is synonymous with what many people think is leadership. This model operates on fear: the team member must perform or we'll remove their ability to pay their mortgage, kids' educational expenses, and so on. Fear pushes people to take action.

However, when driven by fear, human beings generally go to one of three places:

1. They get stuck.
2. They solve problems that don't exist.
3. They focus on the wrong problem, which is low leverage and doesn't deliver the result they want.

Instead, we're going to teach you the five practices, the SmartTribe Accelerators, that will help you get what you want when you want it. (See figure 1-4.)

These SmartTribe Accelerators—focused, clear, accountable, influential, and sustainable results—are how we foster emotional en-

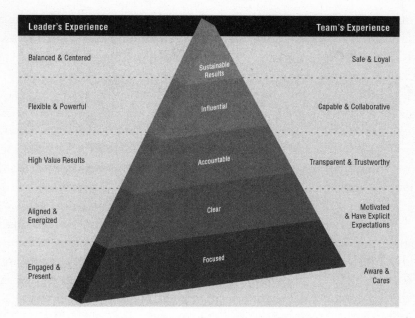

Figure 1-4. The Five SmartTribe Accelerators

gagement and get our team into their Smart State. By using these, we don't have to resort to primeval methods of control and manipulation—which miss our desired outcome anyway. These Accelerators help leaders elevate and cultivate their people. And as a leader cultivates these Accelerators, their experience of personal fulfillment at work increases—as does that of their team members. True leadership inspires people with vision. Vision pulls people not only to take action but also to care about the outcome, to take personal ownership of it, and to bring their "A game" every day.

The team benefits tremendously too. As the leader grows in focus, team members feel the leader is increasingly more aware and cares about them more. As clarity is cultivated, team members feel more motivated and safe since expectations are now explicit. With greater accountability comes an enhanced team member experience of transparency and trustworthiness. As the leader's influence grows, the team members feel the leader is more capable and collaborative. Over time as results are sustained, team members feel safer and more loyal.

So in part 1, you're going to learn why creating a SmartTribe is the key to successfully getting to and through inflection points, and sustainable company growth. Part 2 will cover the key characteristics of

SmartTribes: focus, clarity, accountability, influence, and sustainable results. Part 3 will put it all together with more detailed real-life case studies that will prepare you for the process of change and show you exactly how to create a SmartTribe in your own organization.

It's not just entire companies that build SmartTribes; divisions or teams within a larger company or organization may want their own cohesive SmartTribe too. So whenever I use the word *organization*, especially in terms of "organizational effectiveness," I'm referring to any group that wants its own SmartTribe. I may interchange the word *company* when an entire corporation is becoming a SmartTribe.

After each chapter, I want you to hit the ground running. (Remember, I'm your scout and your coach—not your professor.) At the end of each chapter, I'm going to sum up what we covered in four sections. The Twitter Takeaways will be a quick culling of the key points and practices. The Assess section will enable you to quickly assess where you stand vis-à-vis what you just learned. The Act section will prescribe some actions to take in order to reap the benefits of the ROI section, which will share the results and return on investment our clients have experienced by working through the Assess and Act steps. This format will provide instant opportunities to try these tools, fail fast when needed, and reach results and ROI quickly. Finally, we'll close each chapter with a Resources section that will help you to implement our techniques.

To build and lead a SmartTribe, we need to make sure our people shift from their fear- and safety-driven Critter State to their innovation- and possibility-driven Smart State. How? By ensuring their survival needs are met and they know they belong and are valued. That's the first step in creating a SmartTribe, and the topic of the next chapter. But first, let's take stock of your organization's inflection point status in the sections below.

▼

Twitter Takeaways

Find these helpful? Tweet them to your tribe and reference #SmartTribes as the source. Thanks!

- Organizations travel through relatively predictable revenue inflection points.
- You are either moving up through inflection points or sliding down and losing momentum. Swirling in place is not sustainable.
- At each revenue inflection point, a company must reinvent itself and its people, money strategy, business model.
- How are your sales? What's the process of creating and converting new business? Are your incentive programs working? Are sales commissions tied to profit per sale?
- People are essentially unmanageable—attempts to control and manipulate people will ultimately fail.
- When driven by fear, human beings go to one of three places: 1. They get stuck. 2. They solve problems that don't exist. 3. They focus on the wrong problem, which is low leverage and doesn't deliver the result they want.
- Fear pushes people to take action. Vision pulls people not only to take action but also to care about the outcome.

Assess

Take our Inflection Point Assessment below to determine how ready you are to reach your next revenue inflection point.

Rate yourself on the following questions. Answer each with yes or no, and total your answers at the end.

1. Is your revenue growing as quickly as you want it to?
2. Is your profit growing as quickly as you want it to?
3. Do you have the right people in the right roles doing the right things?
4. Are you retaining your superstar employees?
5. Are you intentionally helping your executive team look into their blind spots, overcome challenging behaviors, and expand their vision and ability to elevate others?
6. Have you identified your next generation of leaders?
7. If so, are you following a specific, proven process to cultivate them?

8. Would you like to get more accountability, communication, and execution from your team?

9. Are you navigating rapid growth or turnaround where internal priorities are frequently shifting and the team is challenged to quickly adapt and stretch?

10. Do you rarely have conflict/backstabbing/silos between departments and/or team members?

11. Does your culture focus more on positive outcomes than negative outcomes?

12. Do you know how to scale and allocate your human resources to get more done with fewer people?

13. Are you keeping your finger on the pulse of the culture and implementing programs to increase emotional equity?

If you have five or more no answers, you're at risk of getting stuck between inflection points.

Look at your score above. What are the key areas where you have the greatest opportunity for growth? Is it in cultivating your culture and team? Increasing or optimizing your revenue? Streamlining your operations?

What inflection point are you headed toward? See figures 1-3a and b, "How to Navigate Common Revenue Inflection Points." Do you have all of the People components from all previous inflection points, plus those for your targeted inflection point, in place?

Act

- Based on your answers above, what three People components can you put in place to ensure you reach your next inflection point?
- What single step can you take toward putting one of these components in place this week?
- Now schedule and complete this action step.

ROI

- If you could add three or more yes answers to the above assessment, what would it be worth to you?

- What results do you think you might get in the first ninety days of implementing your People plan?
- What would they be worth to you?

Resources

Go to www.ChristineComaford.com/resources and download the kits that will be most helpful for you. We think the following kits would be a good start:

- Increasing Accountability and Ensuring Goals Are Met
- Assess Your Team's Performance
- Streamlining Your Sales Funnel
- Leading from the Inside Out
- Optimize Your Daily Operations: Standard Operating Procedures to Streamline Your Operations

2.

THE CONNECTION BETWEEN YOUR
BRAIN AND YOUR CULTURE

So there you are, when suddenly you hear *that song* that reminds you of *that person*. And you're emotionally hijacked—just like that. Good or bad, the song interacts with your neural net and triggers the emotions you have associated with it. Emotional hijacks happen every day, often unconsciously, and often with debilitating results.

An expression on a team member's face subconsciously reminds you of Mom at her most critical, yet you have no idea why you dislike speaking with her. But the team member actually has chronic indigestion, her facial expression has nothing to do with you, and she wonders why you haven't shown her the report, or invited her to the meeting, or told her what's up, or smiled on the way to the coffee machine.

And so it goes. Trigger—response. Trigger—response. Trigger—response. All day, every day. Human beings are meaning-making machines. The trouble is, we often assign meaning where it doesn't exist.

Now, most of these internal programs—the neural connections and associations we make that give experience meaning—are programs we "wrote" between birth and seven years old. Many of our programs either were provided for us by our parents or were coded by our very young and inexperienced reactions to what we perceived as threatening people or situations. Even the most wonderful, well-intentioned parents are going to make a few coding errors. I know I have. I taught my stepson, Spike, that work was hard and stressful. Once I realized that I was contributing to his coding work as difficult, I shifted to re-coding that work is exciting, creates cool opportunities for growth, and that stress really is about fear—and how to get to the bottom of that fear and release it.

Now that we are adults, the question becomes, how can we rewrite our own programs to set the meaning and get the results we want? Further, as leaders, how can we assist others to get the results and experiences they would like? How can we use this knowledge to increase our own and our team's performance, innovation, and engagement?

Let's look at how the Critter State and Smart State would function in a work scenario. Someone takes public credit for your work or throws you under the proverbial bus. Your Critter State gets angry/dejected/terrified, and you either say "This always happens" or "I'll get him/her" or you're stunned and shocked into silence. In your Smart State you'd chose an appropriate stance (more on this in chapter 6) and use the SmartTribe Accelerators of focus and clarity to communicate and influence through the process to reach your desired outcome.

In the coming chapters you're going to learn how to deactivate your own and your team members' fear triggers and to assign appropriate meaning. You're going to learn exactly what to do to create a team that acts as a team, one in which the members support one another and work together to achieve the results you need. A tribe whose culture you created. A SmartTribe of whom you are justifiably proud.

How the Brain Blocks Progress and Performance

Our brains do an amazing and wonderful job, but they don't usually like change very much. You may like the *idea* of change. Parts of you may be very interested in change theory, talking about change, managing change—and especially describing how *other* people should change. However, actual change involving ourselves is scary to certain parts of our brain. The parts that exist to keep us safe have created elegant patterning based on one-trial learning.

Let's take a closer look.

Your brain has three essential parts. The first part—the brain stem—sits at the base of your skull. This part is commonly called the reptilian brain, because it's exactly like the brain of a reptile. It's the oldest and most primitive part of the brain, and it controls balance, temperature regulation, and breathing. It acts out of instinct and is primarily a stimulus-response machine focused on survival.

Layered on top of the brain stem is the mammalian brain, so called because—yep—all the other mammals have this kind of brain too. The mammalian brain controls and expresses emotion, short-term memory, and the body's response to danger. The key player in the mammalian brain that we're going to be talking about in this book is the limbic system, which is the emotional center of the brain, where the fight/flight/freeze response is located. Its primary focus is also survival, though it is also the seat of anger, frustration, happiness, and love.

Let's combine the limbic system with the survival mechanism in the reptilian brain. This creates the powerful combo pack we'll call the *critter brain*, as my mentor Carl Buchheit of NLP Marin[1] terms it. Once our critter brain has equated a particular phenomenon with safety or survival, it will continue to carry out that program. And it will do so as long as we are not dead, because it really doesn't care about our quality of life—it cares about survival. And one key component of staying alive is *belonging*, or being like the other critters in the environment.

Safety and survival are definitely good things, but here's the catch: since our critter brain doesn't care about quality of life, it often will choose behaviors that keep us safe first and foremost. From a survival perspective, detecting threat is more important than being happy. This is why there are more negative than positive words in a language. So if we learn that we can survive by feeling worthless, by becoming invisible, by procrastinating until the last minute and then doing "good enough" work, or even by chronically doing a less-than-stellar job, then that program is the one our critter brain is going to associate with survival. Our brain will keep running that program ad infinitum because it knows we can survive it. Again, survival here means continued breathing. Those old programs are going to run as long as we keep breathing until and unless we can intervene and teach ourselves that something else—maybe even excellence—is not only survivable *but safer*.

Safety, belonging, and mattering are essential to your brain and your ability to perform at work, at home, and in your life overall. The greater the feeling of safety, both mental and physical, the greater the feeling of connection with others, the greater the feeling that we're in this together and we belong together, the greater the feeling that we personally matter and make a difference and are contributing to the greater good, and the greater the success of the organization, the relationship, the team, and the individual.

Let's move on to the third part of the brain: the neocortex. This part of the brain is most evolved in human beings, and the area of it we are most concerned with is the prefrontal cortex. The prefrontal cortex enables us to plan, innovate, solve complex problems, think abstract thoughts, and have visionary ideas. It allows us to measure the quality of our experience, to compare it to an abstract ideal, and to yearn for change. The prefrontal cortex is responsible for a number of advanced behaviors, including social behavior, tool making, language, and higher-level consciousness.

Scientists don't really know all the things this part of the brain is capable of doing, but everyone from quantum physicists to voodoo doctors knows that there is huge untapped potential in the neocortex overall. So we'll leave it at that.

For the purposes of simplicity we'll distill the above to two states: the Critter State, where we don't have access to all parts of our brain and thus are reactive in fight/flight/freeze, running safety programs; and the Smart State, where we have easy access to all of our resources and can respond from choice. (See figures 2-1 and 2-2 below.)

Today, innovation and growth through the next revenue inflection point depend on making sure the Smart State, not the Critter State, is driving management decisions and behavior in relationships. Management practices that rely on fear to enforce compliance keep people in their Critter State, in old safety and survival patterns, and reduce innovation. We need to get our teams into the Smart State, where they create new neural patterns for what it means to fail or succeed. Or, as Brené Brown puts it in her book *Daring Greatly*, "If we want to reignite innovation and passion, we have to rehumanize work. When shame becomes a management style, engagement dies. When failure is not an option we can forget about learning, innovation, and creativity."[2] The management practice of keeping people in their Critter State has grown not only increasingly obsolete but also increasingly ineffective.

Now, the Critter State is still useful, of course, and we want it to take over if a car is careening out of control and heading for us. We also will use it to engage emotionally. We simply want to make sure that we have full access to all parts of our brain so we are in both positive emotion and positive momentum.

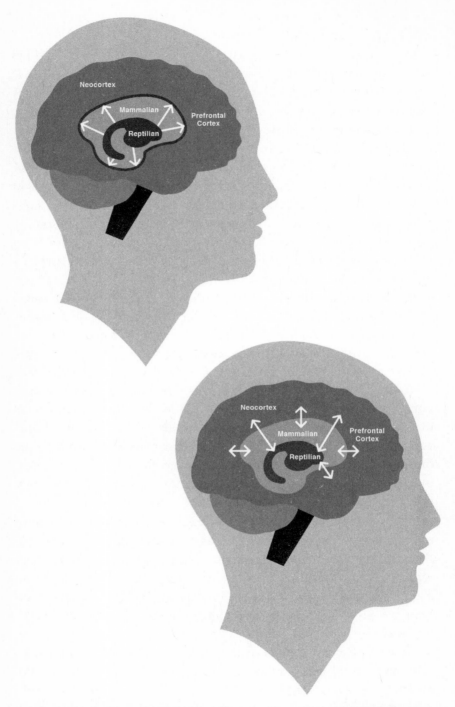

Figure 2-1 (top). Critter State: Limited Access to Resources. Figure 2-2 (bottom). Smart State: Full Access to Resources

Stuck Spot: The Invisible Adviser

Let's look at a common case of the Critter State winning over the Smart State: the performance hijack. Performance hijacks happen when people lose their access to resources in clutch situations. For example, a high-potential manager walks into a senior manager's office and can't speak in coherent sentences although he knows the material. Or a seasoned executive babbles at the board meeting when she is known for her clear thinking. Or the manager who just saved the company has been asked to present what he did and flounders through the presentation. All these are examples of a critter brain that has hijacked the prefrontal cortex.

Alex is a client of ours who works for a prestigious worldwide consulting group. He had been promoted to a role that involved far more presenting to and persuading key clients, and suddenly he was freezing, stumbling, and losing clients. This high performer had become a liability. What was happening to Alex?

We all have patterning that at one time in our lives was vital for survival and/or belonging. In Alex's case, his patterning was to be as invisible as possible; he'd been wired in childhood to avoid a parent with a rage problem. Invisibility was equivalent to safety for young Alex. The current-day trigger of high visibility in front of important clients kept plunging him into his Critter State, where he had learned to shrink from the world in order to survive. His Critter State was running the show to ensure his survival while his Smart State was shut down.

I am using Alex's case here to illustrate what can happen when neural wiring starts running amok. All behaviors and behavior patterns had some kind of intended positive outcome at the time they were created; they were useful in some way to help the individual get the positive outcome he or she sought. The trouble is that as we grow and change, some behavior patterns no longer serve us. They either need to be updated for the well-being of our current selves or, as in Alex's case, they need to be released entirely. Adult Alex was no longer under daily physical threat, so it was essential to teach his brain that he would be safer being visible.

Another client panicked when asked to speak in front of a group (*group* being defined as more than one person). Another client inexplicably age-regressed and took on the behavior of a young child in front of a new board member. Yet another client wanted new financing but consistently sabotaged new opportunities. Performance hijacks, all—and more common than you may think. Per Dr. Howard Rankin, our Critter State hijacks our Smart State often—and usually within one-twelfth of a second!

I am happy to report that the tools you'll learn about in part 2 of this book work extremely well in helping your tribe to access their resourceful Smart State in most business situations. In Alex's case, we also applied a process that allowed him to have choices about his behaviors in formerly triggering high-visibility situations. Here's essentially what the process was: we excavated the initial trauma that had created the invisibility safety pattern. Next, we helped him access resources he already applied in other contexts, including quick analysis of a situation and clearly articulating his point of view. Then we connected and anchored these helpful resources to the problem state (the hijack trigger) so he was able to use a new path of response as opposed to his historical and compulsive reaction. He has now been promoted (again!) to partner and capably persuades clients to follow new strategies and buy more of his company's services.

When performance hijacks happen, our Critter State is trying to keep us safe by running an old program that worked once—meaning that we survived that original situation. Cases of hijack include anything that triggers an automatic reaction that we would not consciously choose.

The Critter State will always trump the Smart State. Survival will always be coded as paramount. The trick is to increase safety, belonging, and mattering. When we do that, when we even make it safe for our team to recognize when they are triggered and to step back from it, we increase choice, allow change, and promote innovation.

Fear Pushes, Vision Pulls

If we look at the management techniques that emerged in the Industrial Revolution, they seem far more based on Critter State phenomena than on Smart State evolution. Survival was based on driving your competition into the ground and the law of the sea prevailed: the bigger fish wins.

If your competition was in-house, if the culture of the company encouraged you to compete against your own side, this was considered okay. The theory was, if you competed against each other, you would work harder for the company. If the culture was a bit cutthroat, well, that was just the price of higher performance.

Then came the Information Age, and we were faced with increasing complexity of tasks and accelerating technological innovation. Holding people in fear and driving them into the unresourceful and highly stressful Critter State just doesn't work anymore. Fear may push people to action, but this approach is not sustainable and will ultimately lead to either burnout or extreme apathy. The imagining of a new, better future where there are compelling rewards pulls, attracts, and draws people forward, and emotionally engages them. With vision, the Smart State is engaged, and we can create, love what we're doing, work longer hours, and leave work excited and wanting to come back for more. Technically, engagement, excitement, and passion reside in the right hemisphere of the brain, primarily in the temporal lobe. The limbic system includes areas of the cortex and the inner-facing parts of the temporal, frontal, and parietal lobes. This system acts as a connector by being a link between higher consciousness (Smart State) in the cortex and the reptilian brain that manages the body's physical responses (Critter State). What is key is that with a SmartTribe we have the synthesis of the "smart" and "emotional + safety" brain—and thus get the best of both.

Growth Mindset

It is time for leaders to learn how to be agile, how to fail fast, how to learn to live in their Smart State—and guide their teams there too.

Unfortunately, many of us have been socialized differently. We were given tests at school that decided how smart we were. We were taught that intelligence is fixed, or that some people have talent because they are born with it. Many who were told that they were smart have spent their lifetimes defending that identity by never taking any risks. If you don't try anything new, you can't fail, and no one can challenge your perception of being "the smart kid."

But what is *smart*, really? Is it IQ, high grades, and college degrees, or is it the ability to adapt, to be resilient, to persevere in the face of adversity, and to seek challenge, learning, and growth? Is it being rigid, or is it being flexible and changeable?

According to Carol Dweck, author of *Mindset: The New Psychology of Success*, we can succeed if we embrace a growth mindset.[3] Simply put, we can improve anything, but—and this is a pretty big *but*—we have to want it and work at it. This means we have to not only learn to accept failure and feedback, *we have to seek it.* It's how we handle failure that determines our success. Do we get every bit of information we can and use it to try again? Do we work hard and keep practicing to overcome our limitations? That's what Michael Jordan did when he was cut from the high school basketball team—and how he became one of the greatest basketball players of all time.

Nowadays it's the *smarter* fish that win over the bigger fish. The smarter fish have the tools and the ability to manage and shift their and their team's Critter States into Smart States.

A Visual Guide to the Critter and Smart States

We are all mostly familiar with the idea of a country having a "culture." We might even think of some stereotypes: French people have sensitive culinary palates and wear berets; Italian people like pasta and have great design; Americans eat hamburgers and are known for baseball and toothy grins. Now, if you actually walk around in France, Italy, or America, you will find that a large portion of the French population does not wear berets, plenty of Italians dislike pasta, and there are even Americans who have small teeth and neither play nor watch baseball.

However, those cultural stereotypes exist because there are enough people for whom this applies so that it appears de rigueur in that culture. Likewise, an organization evolves cultural norms—beliefs about how the world works and what is "normal." The composite of these norms creates an identity. So if team members yelling at or disrespecting one another, gossiping, and public beheadings are considered normal, then you may be dealing with a Critter State, fear-driven company culture. If healthy conflict, respectful disagreement, and productive feedback are normal, you are well on your way to a SmartTribe culture.

If you are thinking, *Uh-oh, there's way too much fear in my culture*, let me give you a few quick tips on how to turn that around. The first method is to teach yourself and your team a hand signal that serves the dual purpose of explaining the Critter State hijack phenomenon and also lets you signal to one another when it's happening. We're going to use your hand to represent your brain in this technique learned from the brilliant Dr. Daniel J. Siegel.[4]

Hold one of your hands up, palm out, and cross your thumb over it. Like this:

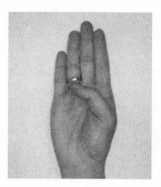

The base of your palm represents your brain stem, or your reptilian brain. Your palm represents your mammalian brain, with your thumb representing your limbic system. Now fold your fingers over your thumb and make a fist.

The back of your hand and fingers represent your neocortex, with your knuckles to fingertips representing your prefrontal cortex. Your closed fist represents full access to all parts of your brain, from your prefrontal cortex through your reptilian brain. This is your Smart State—where you have great choice, you're creative, present, emotionally engaged, and ready to roll.

Now think of the last time you "flipped your lid"—you had a tough day, you got triggered, and you dived into your critter brain and were in fight/flight/freeze. This is where you were:

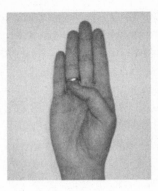

Your Smart State was hijacked and your Critter State was running the show. In this case your undesired (by your conscious decision making) safety patterns were in charge and you didn't have access to resourceful states. Your frontal lobes were flapping in the breeze, using their time- and pattern-matching capabilities to trigger Critter State activity and access to "negative" states like anxiety. (We don't really like to judge these states as positive or negative, because every state has a use in some context, but these states are undesirable when you don't have access to the resources you need to solve a problem or move forward.)

Now once again close your fingers over your thumb—like the victory punch people throw in the air when they are successful. Like this:

As I mentioned above, this is going to symbolize full access to the resources in your frontal lobes through your reptilian brain. Remember, access to the frontal lobes' resources allows you to plan, innovate, solve complex problems, think abstract thoughts, have visionary ideas, experience higher consciousness, and love—to be in your Smart State.

Be sure to teach these hand signals to your team, as they are super helpful to use at work. When I am really stressed out, I'll show the "flip your lid" signal above. When I'm in a meeting and want everyone to be in their "creative zone," I'll show the closed-hand symbol. Table 2-1 is a quick reference guide for some behaviors that send us into our Critter State versus our Smart State (note that all the Smart State behaviors are taught in this book).

Note that some roles with either high routine or high stress—such as those in data entry, assembly lines, and call centers—are more apt to see workers slide into their Critter State. This is where cultural rituals in which team members are recognized for their contributions as well as a highly emotional mission, vision, and set of values help tremendously. More on both of these in parts 2 and 3.

I hope by now you're convinced that the Smart State is better for business, especially a business where innovation and change are necessary for growth. It's also the optimal state to lead people from, to sell from, to grow from, to live from. It's all about the Smart State.

TABLE 2-1. BEHAVIORS THAT SEND US INTO OUR CRITTER STATE AND SMART STATE

What sends us into our Critter State	What sends us into our Smart State
Layoffs/reorganizations without explanation	Clear messaging on what this layoff or reorganization means and how it is for the health of the company and team
Tight/unrealistic deadlines	A culture of promises and requests, clear priorities, and safety in communication
Conflict	A culture that supports differing opinions and acknowledges plus resolves conflict openly
Gossip	Zero tolerance for gossip, with full leadership support
Political posturing	Zero tolerance for politics, backstabbing, sabotage, and undermining, with full leadership support
Secrecy/the unknown	Consistent and transparent communication
Mixed messages/unclear expectations	Explicit communication and needle movers that spell out expectations and goals
Budget cuts	Clear messaging on "belt tightening" and how we can all chip in
Imposed change	Clear change messaging with an explanation as to why and what it means
Revenue loss/key customer loss	Clear messaging on how we'll turn this around
Burnout	Sustainable cultures with managed workloads

▼

Twitter Takeaways

Find these helpful? Tweet them to your tribe and reference #Smart-Tribes as the source. Thanks!

- Human beings have two primary areas of their brains: what we call the critter brain, which is the part of us that reacts with fight/flight/freeze and is primarily concerned with safety; and the prefrontal cortex, where we can choose to respond, innovate, and grow.
- The critter brain will trump the prefrontal cortex until we learn tools to manage our emotional state and get unstuck.
- To grow our business and navigate to and through revenue inflection points we must spend as much time as possible in our Smart State, and create structures for our team to do the same.
- Human beings are meaning-making machines. The neural connections and associations we make that give experience meaning are programs we "wrote" between birth and seven years old.
- Safety, belonging, and mattering are essential to your brain and your ability to perform at work, at home, and in your life overall.
- The imagining of a new, better future where there are compelling rewards pulls, attracts, and draws people forward, and emotionally engages them.
- What is *smart*, really? Is it IQ, high grades, college degrees, or the ability to adapt, to be resilient, to persevere in the face of adversity, and to seek challenge, learning, and growth?
- Nowadays it's the *smarter* fish that win over the bigger fish. The smarter fish have the tools and the ability to manage and shift their and their team's Critter States into Smart States.

Assess

- What percentage of time do you spend in your Smart State versus your Critter State in your work? In your life overall?
- Consider your company organizational chart. Starting at the top, what percentage of time do you think your C-suite spends in their Smart State versus their Critter State? How about the executive team? The management team? The supervisory level? The individual contributors?
- Now consider your culture overall. What percentage of your culture's working time is spent in the Smart State? The Critter State?
- What behaviors do you and your company leadership have that might send someone into their Critter State?

Act

- What are three things you could do this week to help foster a greater sense of safety, open communication, and risk taking within your team and colleagues? Setting standard meeting and communication rhythms is a great start, as is looking into roles, responsibilities, and accountability structures. When people know what they are responsible for, how to deliver it, and who they can turn to for help, safety is increased.
- What are three things you could do this week to help foster a greater sense of belonging, connection, and camaraderie within your team and colleagues? We find that team brainstorming, cross-functional task forces with a common goal, and team victory celebrations are a good start.
- What are three things you could do this week to help foster a greater sense of mattering, recognition, and appreciation within your team and colleagues? We find that daily appreciation of one or more team members is a solid start. (Be sure to be specific about what you like!) Individual needle movers (see chapter 5) that clearly contribute to the company's needle movers are very powerful too.

ROI

- What results will your tasks in the Act section above yield in the first 90 days? In the first 120 days?
- How will you measure your ROI? See chapter 14 for the results we recommend tracking for your SmartTribe.

Resources

Go to www.ChristineComaford.com/resources and download the kits that will be most helpful for you. We think the following kits would be a good start:

- Leading from the Inside Out
- Increasing Accountability and Ensuring Goals Are Met
- Assess Your Team's Performance

Also check out the following in the appendix:

- Presence Process
- Silence Practice Techniques
- Energy Recall

PART TWO

THE FIVE SMARTTRIBE ACCELERATORS

3.

FOCUS
Bright Shiny Objects Are Not *Your Friends*

I n order to make any change, personal, professional, or organizational, you have to know where you currently stand. It's not sexy. It's not fun. But you have to do it. At Christine Comaford Associates (CCA) we start every client engagement with some form of assessment. Sometimes it's a Leadership Assessment, sometimes we ask a bunch of informal questions on a call, and sometimes we use a Cultural Assessment, where we interview a relevant sample of a team and uncover shortcuts and roadblocks to growth. We recommend that if you are aiming to change something, you enlist the support of a trusted adviser, because it's almost impossible to see what's going on from inside.

Here's what can happen if you don't: the blame game starts, and the next thing you know you're on the precipitous inflection point death spiral—heading downward instead of in the up direction that you want.

SmartTribe Accelerator #1: Focus

The single most important practice in creating a SmartTribe is to know where you are and be where you are: to focus. Practicing focus has three dimensions. The first dimension of focus is to be *present* with people here and now. This means that if you are at a meeting, you are listening to what people are saying and not thinking about the past or the future. The second dimension of focus is to be *real* about where you are, to make a clear distinction between envisioning an outcome and wishful thinking. The third dimension of focus is to *prioritize* high-value (strategic or "top down") activities and *manage* low-value (distracting or "bottom up") time wasters.

When you are focused you feel engaged and present and your team feels that you are aware and you care. Practicing focus is a foundational skill, the primary SmartTribe Accelerator. It's the first chapter in part 2 because it underpins all the rest. This chapter is mostly about the first two dimensions of focus (*present* and *real*), but we'll talk more about the third (*prioritization*) and how you can get back five to fifteen hours per week when we talk about Needle Movers in chapter 5, so stay tuned.

Let's start with a case of what can go wrong when you don't focus.

Our Brain's Filtering System:
Deletion, Distortion, and Generalization

The human brain deletes, distorts, and generalizes our world every second of every day. It has to, or we would go crazy from the amount of input we'd have to process—which is exactly what happens in bipolar and some psychotic disorders. The thalamus, the brain's filter for deletion, allows too much input to reach the processing parts of the brain. This leads to great creativity—and in the extreme, to insanity.

Take deleting. If we didn't have the filter that deleting provides, we would be fully conscious of every input and every factoid we came across every nanosecond. Right now as I am typing, my brain is busy deleting the sounds of traffic and a ticking clock, the arrival of the postal carrier, and the fact that likely ten or more e-mails have come in since last I checked and some of them might require immediate action—this is good, healthy, sane deletion.

The problem comes when we delete what we don't want to see, hear, feel, or deal with. Perhaps you have an aging parent and you're deleting your concern for their future—you'll deal with it later, and then you'll plan their estate and where and how they'll spend their final days. Perhaps you're deleting that your personal assistant still didn't do what you asked and you'll have to give her feedback on her incomplete work. These kinds of deletions—denials, actually—are unhealthy and energy draining if they continue too long and become procrastination. In organizations, executives sometimes delete the real problems and focus instead on trivia.

Distorting is helpful in that it enables us to feel and react to our world. If we didn't feel more strongly about certain things rather than others, we'd be automatons. We wouldn't know what is important. The feelings that distortions provide give us feedback and a way to know how to prioritize. Our ability to give more attention to situation X means that situation Y has lower priority. That's okay if situation X is the fire we must fight right now.

We also distort, blow out of proportion, or obsess about anger, fear, or the consequences of expressing our feelings. Anyone who has witnessed a teenager's response to not being asked to the prom, being stood up for a date, or suffering some other social pain ("It's the *end of the world*! I'll never be able to face Taylor/Ashley/whomever again. I can't go back to school!") has seen some unhealthy distortion. Business distortions come when we focus disproportionally on something that is not really the issue—for example, one dropped ball amid ninety-nine that were knocked out of the park (and often the dropped ball wasn't even essential).

We generalize too, thank goodness. If we didn't, we'd have to learn how to turn on the lights in every room we walked into instead of knowing how a switch works and that one is similar to another. Generalization serves a purpose in that it enables us to assume consistency in our world. Were all rooms and lighting scenarios considered different, we'd waste tremendous amounts of energy constantly learning how to navigate our world.

Generalization goes wrong when we assume we know what we don't. We've all had moments of believing "this always happens," "they always act that way," or "here we go again." When we project reality based on what didn't work previously, we don't allow for anything to change. Being present means focusing on the possibility in that current moment.

Deletion, distortion, and generalization are all key components of being present to our world and the situations and people around us. But we need to make sure our natural filtering system filters out only the things that don't have to be addressed right now and doesn't filter out the present moment. Where is your focus right now? How present are you right now? Do you have a little voice in your head right now listing all the things you need to do today, tomorrow, and next week?

Being present means being here, focusing on now, and nowhere else. Not in the past, not in the future. Just here. Being present means looking at your world, your situation, your team, your concerns or fears, your intentions, your beliefs, and your commitments. Being present is essential to lead, to feel emotionally engaged, and to help your team feel you are aware of the key issues.

Why is being present sometimes hard? Because being truly here sometimes hurts, or sometimes means we need to deal with things we have been avoiding. The more we can address an issue the moment we perceive it, the calmer and more present we are, and the easier it is for others to follow our lead.

How to Get and Stay Focused in the Now

To be present we have to know what we want to create in an interaction or meeting, and focus on what is actually happening now so that we can correct our course.

If we are repeatedly avoiding something or if we feel like a pattern keeps recurring, chances are there is an "intended positive outcome" to not being present. For example, if we repeatedly avoid confronting a subordinate, it is probably because it feels better and safer not to.

It feels better not only in that moment but also retroactively in all the other times that you avoided something and survived it. Our brain is wired to keep us safe, and once it learns one way of keeping us safe, it generalizes and continues to keep us safe in just that way. Yet this keeps us in our Critter State—and not our Smart State. Changing that pattern and learning to be present with conflict means that we have to understand the parts of us that want to run away. These parts are just keeping us safe. Instead of fighting them or making them wrong, we can accept them, even honor them (continuing to breathe is generally a good thing, yes?), and then retrain ourselves to have choice. We can always avoid things (if we really want to), but to lead we have to have the choice and the preference to address most situations in the present.

One of the best ways to get and stay present is to focus on how you are increasing safety (and encouraging people to take risks), belonging (and a "We're all in this together, we're the same" experience), and mattering ("It matters that *you*, specifically, are here; I see your unique gifts") in each interaction you have. With this focus, the constant parade of bright shiny distractions has less ability to pull your attention away. You'll also avoid boredom (which pulls us away from being present) because you'll be focusing on the fascinating person you're interacting with. And everyone, I promise, is fascinating in some way. One extra benefit to remember: safety + belonging + mattering = trust.

Inquiry Fosters Presence

Being present also means using inquiry over advocacy. Most of us leaders have an itchy trigger finger. A team member asks us how to do something, and we rattle off the answer; we advocate. What is the result of this? We develop order takers. We train people to ask instead of figuring it out on their own—which keeps them in their Critter State and prevents us from being truly present with them. We're so busy planning our answer, our order, our advocacy, that we miss an opportunity to connect and to cultivate leadership (and safety, belonging, and mattering, to boot!).

What would happen if we inquired instead, if we asked them how they would do it? What impact their course of action might have? Yes, we'd have to shut up and let our team members think it through, and the first few times might be excruciatingly slow, but then—oh, yes—they would become leaders. They'd stop seeking excessive direction and approval because they'd *own* their area.[1]

Here's how it works. You'll likely do three inquiry sessions with someone before they start to expect you to ask questions versus give orders. Next, they'll come to you with ideas (since they know you'll inquire anyway) and they'll seek feedback and validation. After a few of these feedback/validation sessions, they'll then come to you saying they have a plan: here it is, speak now if you aren't okay with it. Then next—voilà—they won't come to you since they'll have taken ownership of their area.

Did you note the best part? Your inquiry created a sense of safety, belonging, and mattering. You just took a small and important step toward creating a SmartTribe.

Stuck Spot: Feuding Founders

At certain inflection points, one common phenomenon is that the partners who grew a company together start to feud and run the risk of completely destroying what they have built.

Roberta is a CEO at a mid-sized automotive parts company. She and her business partner, Greg, blew through the first few inflection points and rapidly grew their company. True to form, nearing the $100 million mark, they began to have some serious disagreements. They each had clear responsibilities, but Roberta kept diving into Greg's area, offering direction to his team, changing decisions and policies Greg had set, and generally causing confusion. Roberta was avoiding a direct discussion with Greg about performance and accountability.

Diagnosis: Neither was practicing any of the three dimensions of focus.

They were both avoiding their need to change (people, money, and model . . . remember?). They were at an inflection point, and what had made them successful so far was not going to take them to the next level.

Greg saw Roberta's micromanagement as an attack. Instead of directly confronting her with his interpretation of her behavior, Greg began to withhold information, causing trouble for Roberta and resulting in awkward moments at board meetings. Roberta in turn felt attacked and exacerbated the problem by recruiting the loyalties of key board and team members. Not being present, or deflecting or avoiding structural issues, is a key symptom of getting stuck at an inflection point.

When we were brought in, the first goal was to assess the damage to the culture and people, and then to make peace between Roberta and Greg. During our Cultural Assessment process, we took an in-depth look at how their culture was functioning. We learned that the division among the team was significantly deeper than we had been led to believe. In fact, we found that three key executives were ready to quit—they couldn't succeed and grow their career in a war zone. Further, we found poor to mediocre performance and countless errors in both accounting (Greg's area) and quality assurance (Roberta's area). Morale was in the gutter.

Roberta and Greg had no idea how their divisiveness was affecting others. They thought it was a small problem between the two of them—not a major symptom of systemic dysfunction.

Looking closely at the cultural wounds their behavior created resulted not only in a plan of action to address these issues but also in key players feeling heard and increasing their confidence in team leadership. They began an internal leadership program to retain and develop these key executives. And these executives passed on the training they received to their teams, helping to shift team members from the role of Victim to that of Outcome Creator (more on this in chapter 8).

Both Roberta and Greg received personal coaching: first to notice, or to be present with, what they were actually doing, and later to understand how what they were doing was serving their own sense of safety but not the company's. Greg and Roberta took to heart the "inquiry over advocacy" idea and immediately applied it. Greg quickly saw that Roberta had the company's best interests at heart, and Roberta soon stopped micromanaging because she no longer felt the need to. They learned how to be more real with each other and mapped out some new strategic initiatives together.

Within four months the Roberta-Greg battle had ended. Within six months Greg was in a new, more appropriate role with a fresh new focus, and the entire organizational chart had been revamped and optimized. Within fifteen months of dedicated and constant commitment to behavior change, the entire company had become aligned, profits had hit a new record, and leadership was a common daily topic across all levels of the company. Roberta and Greg now work together very well, and the company is one cohesive team.

The company quickly grew past the $100 million inflection point, where a whole new set of people, money, and model opportunities arose. They plan on passing the $250 million inflection point within three years.

Twitter Takeaways

Find these helpful? Tweet them to your tribe and reference #SmartTribes as the source. Thanks!

- Our brains delete, distort, and generalize. This filtering system is a good thing, but we need to make sure it filters out only what doesn't need to be addressed now. Be clear on what you need to focus on now and what you want to ditch, delegate, or defer. This will make all the difference.
- Where is your focus right now? How present are you right now? Do you have a little voice in your head right now listing all the things you need to do today, tomorrow, and next week?
- How are you increasing safety (and encouraging people to take risks), belonging (a "We're all in this together, we're the same" experience), and mattering ("It matters that *you*, specifically, are here") in each interaction you have?
- Leaders sometimes delete the real problems and focus instead on trivia. What are you focusing on?
- One of the best ways to get and stay present is to focus on how you are increasing safety, belonging, mattering with your team.
- What would happen if you asked questions (inquired) instead of gave orders (advocated)?
- Inquiry builds leaders—advocacy builds order takers. Five inquiries per advocacy!
- Safety + belonging + mattering = trust.

Assess

List three things you may not be present to in both your business and your personal life. Examples are a strategy for scaling your finance department that is today only barely keeping up, a plan for your aging parents, and so on.

- What is the "cost" or risk of not being present to these things?
- When do you need to become present to them?

Act

- This week, experiment with five inquiries per advocacy. For each order you give ask five questions to start mentoring your team members to find their own solutions. You'll be amazed at how often you rattle off orders and later complain that your people are order takers.

- Take the list of three things you aren't being present to in both your business and your personal life. Take one item in each category and either do it, ditch it, delegate it, or defer it so you no longer have it tugging at your attention in the background.

ROI

- Track the amount of time you've spent excessively managing people (e.g., advocating). You'll note that once you switch to inquiry you'll start to gain more hours each week to do what you want—more strategic/interesting work and less directing of others.
- Our clients see the following results when they practice inquiry. This is reason enough to change one's behavior!
  - ◆ 97% tangibly contribute to increasing key executive strategic/high-value time by five to fifteen hours per week.
  - ◆ Individuals are 67–100% more emotionally engaged, loyal, accountable, and ownership-focused.

Resources

Helpful resources in this chapter include the following:

- The three dimensions of focus
- Inquiry versus advocacy

Go to www.ChristineComaford.com/resources and download the kits that will be most helpful for you. We think the following kits would be a good start:

- Leading from the Inside Out
- Special Report: The Five Critical Mistakes That Halt CEOs

- Assess Your Team's Performance
- Optimize Your Daily Operations: Standard Operating Procedures to Streamline Your Operations

Also check out the following in the appendix:

- Presence Process
- Silence Practice Techniques
- Energy Recall

CLARITY
Stealing Underpants Isn't Enough

4.

My favorite *South Park* episode is called "Gnomes."[1] Here's the gist of the story, as I remember it.

Tweek's underpants are being stolen. He has only one pair left.

Tweek invites the boys to sleep over and catch the thieves in the act. In the wee hours of the morning, the boys spot a gnome sneaking into Tweek's bedroom and stealing his last pair of underpants.

"Why are you stealing my underpants?" Tweek shrieks. "That's my last pair!"

The gnome replies, "It's all part of our business plan." The boys accept the gnome's invitation to follow him to his headquarters and learn about their business.

When the boys arrive at the gnomes' headquarters they see piles and piles of underpants, all shapes, sizes, colors, and styles. They are heaped in huge piles everywhere. Gnomes scurry to and fro, pushing enormous carts of underpants around.

"What are you doing with all these underpants?" the boys ask.

The gnome confidently replies, "Oh, this is just the collection phase: Phase 1."

"What is Phase 2?" Now the boys are getting really curious.

The gnome doesn't know, so he introduces them to the CEO gnome, who fires up a PowerPoint presentation.

"We have a three-step plan for our business," the CEO gnome proudly says as he clicks to the first slide. It says, "Phase 1: Collect Underpants."

He clicks for Phase 2, which we see has no strategy—just a giant question mark. Phase 2 is blank.

He clicks again for Phase 3, and the slide reads, "Phase 3: Profit!!!" The gnomes cheer as the CEO reads this last step aloud. There is much rejoicing.

Too bad the gnomes will never reach Phase 3. Without Phase 2, they're toast.

Sound familiar?

Compelling Vision or Vague Concept?

How many loyal workers go about their business but have no idea why they do what they do? The gnomes themselves do not understand their own business plan, or why they steal underpants. This is identical to a business where team members do not understand the vision or how to contribute to it. That business, just like the Underpants Gnomes Underwear Enterprise, will never move to the next inflection point—not for all the underpants in the world.

We have a clarity issue here; how exactly do we move from stealing underpants to profit? That's key—that's really *all* that matters to get to the gnomes' endgame. As it stands they simply have a cave full of underpants. No sales, marketing, distribution, target market, merchandising, you name it.

Profit? That's a pipe dream. Ain't gonna happen.

Do you know your company vision? Do your team members know it? Do they feel emotional about it?

The answer to those three questions can stall a company's ability to create a SmartTribe and stunt their growth at the current inflection point. When my team does a Cultural Assessment at a company, often the first questions we ask each of the interviewees are about the company vision and their alignment with it. We're not looking to see if the vision is almighty and powerful. We're looking to see if there is one at all, if people can articulate it in their own words, and if they are engaged by it. We're looking for *clarity*. It's that simple . . . and yet that difficult.

SmartTribe Accelerator #2: Clarity

Clarity is crucial in both vision and communication. Clarity can also be an act of omission—what we choose to be explicit and implicit about. This choice sets up the person we're interacting with to succeed or struggle—and sometimes this person is oneself.

Being clear is essential to leading. When we're clear we feel aligned and energized, and our team feels motivated because they have explicitly stated expectations. So why is being clear sometimes hard? Because being truly clear means we need to take the time to discover what we need, to articulate it clearly, and to be sure the other party understood our communication.

The meaning of the communication is what the other party understood, not what you said, or intended to say, or "really meant." You are responsible for making sure that the receiver understood, and if they didn't, to try, try again.

Clarity has three domains:

- Clarity of our words (saying what we truly mean or expressing what we truly need)
- Clarity of our vision and plan (where we are now, where we want to go, and how we are going to get there)
- Clarity of our intentions and energy (embodying and modeling the outcomes we want for our team)

Clarity of Our Words

Clarity of our words requires us to increase explicit communication and expectations and decrease implicit communication and expectations. Explicit expectations are stated outright—we know exactly what is expected of us in detail ("Please e-mail me a spreadsheet of our top five manufacturing suppliers, who the vendors are, our payment terms, and all payment-related contract terms by 5 P.M. Friday, June 15"). Implicit expectations are those that we figure our team member will magically "figure out" ("Please send me a report of our top manufacturing expenses and the details of each." By when? In what file format? Digital or printed? What exact details do you want?). You can't expect someone to know what you mean unless you tell them, and low or vague information often sends people into their Critter State.

Perhaps you recall that in the last chapter I encouraged you to use inquiry (guiding people to lead) instead of advocacy (command and control) in order to stay present. Here's a great inquiry question to put in your tool kit:

"What specifically do you mean by that?"

Or variations, such as: How specifically will you do that / will that happen? Who specifically will want to buy that? What specifically does _____ mean?

This very simple-seeming question is extraordinarily useful and often omitted on mission-critical items. Note that in the case of the Underpants Gnomes, none of the gnomes asked what specifically Phase 2 was until the kids showed up. So how were they going to get to the "Profit!!!" part?

Try out this question when you think you know the answer. You'll be surprised by how often your assumptions are inaccurate, or at least by how much more you learn by asking.

Clarity of Our Vision and Plan

In my previous book, *Rules for Renegades*, I talked about how an MBA is optional but a GSD (Get Stuff Done) is essential. To ensure you reach the next inflection point it helps to make your brand equal results. Mastering the skill of clarity in terms of communicating your vision and plan is crucial so your team will know where you are now, where you want to go, and how you plan to get there.

For example, the Underpants Gnomes would've benefited from a plan that included exactly how, once collected, the underpants would be marketed and distributed to retail/web/catalog outlets, how orders would be fulfilled, how annual revenue targets would be achieved, what the costs of goods sold would be, and more in order to get to their glorious profit goal.

To take this a step further, a clear mission, vision, and values statement will grab hold of your team's emotions and provide motivation to excel. Of course, part of effective communication is structural clarity, but it helps if your statement is brief or exciting.

Together we'll tease apart your organization's mission, vision, and values in order to get something that is useful for your organization. The test of something "useful" is if it crosses two contexts:

- Professional: Does it achieve what the organization needs in order to succeed?
- Personal: Does it really capture our heart, inspire us to exist, and fuel our passion?

We'll start with the assumption that we all want to be effective, both within the organization and within ourselves. And let's define *effective* as creating the results we want long-term and with sustainability. To be effective, we need to be clear about our mission, vision, and values.

Mission, Vision, and Values Defined

Mission. Peter Senge, past director of the Center for Organizational Learning at the MIT Sloan School of Management, and author of *The Fifth Discipline*,[2] defines the word *mission* as the "why." Why are we in business? Why are we doing what we do here? Why does this organization exist? If you look across contexts, you could ask the same question about yourself as a person, or as a couple, or as a family. Consider the Constitution of the United States, where the preamble states, "We the people of the United States, in order to form a more perfect union, establish justice, ensure domestic tranquility . . ." Got it. This is the mission.

The Constitution explicitly states the mission of the country hundreds of years later. Your mission is a long-term proposition that is lasting—that doesn't change.

Vision. Vision is a little different. A vision is a picture of what you want, as far out on the horizon as you can see, as an organization or as an individual. This can be three to five years, or even longer. Regardless of what works for you, it's wise to keep your vision far enough out to see the goal long-term while also making decisions supporting it today, and allowing room to revise it.

Examples include the Manhattan Project's vision that war would be eliminated with the use of their bomb because the human cost would be so great that no one would want to go to war, and John F. Kennedy's vision of putting a man on the moon in ten years. If our mission is our "why," our vision is our "what."

Values. Values determine standards of behavior, the code of conduct that you will not compromise. The values are the "how" to the "what" of the vision—they are in service to both the mission and the vision. Your values are what you honor and believe in, which will govern how you will behave as you are fulfilling your mission and creating your vision.

Mission Drill Down

Let's start the discussion with questions:

Why are we here as an organization? Why do we exist?

or

What are we going to create that will not have existed without our being here? What are we going to make happen because we exist?

In answering these questions your mission will be clear. Loop in your executive team when clarifying your mission. And once you have it, know you'll refine over time. This is not about getting things perfect, because they will never be perfect. And what is "perfect" anyway, other than a conversation about how we are not good enough? Isn't it better to have a conversation about what we have and how it can empower us to create cool things?

Although we are not looking at our personal mission at this time, you should keep it in mind as you progress through defining your corporate mission. Can you achieve your personal mission within the organization? Sometimes people tell me their personal mission is to "make a lot of money." Well, you can throw that out. Because there are a million ways to make a lot of money, and that is not why you are with this team, in this city, engaged in this opportunity—you are here for something much bigger. Money is simply a by-product. If we all pull together as a team and support the four factors of a sustainable SmartTribe (we'll cover this in chapter 10), money is inevitable. So ask yourself what your mission truly is.

Vision Drill Down

If we stick with our original definition that a vision is a clear picture you can see of the organization, as far out as you can see on the horizon, ask yourself the following questions to craft your vision:

What's the clear future you see for the organization?

and

What do you want your world to be like / to have achieved in the future?

Vision can be distilled through these questions, or we can ask ourselves in the opposite way: what are we willing to give up to have alignment on what the future looks like? Often, having a clear vision is challenging, because we look at only what we want; however, we know that in our lives, often what we want and what we end up with can be different. Mostly that difference is the summation of our behaviors and actions along the way. So, it can be very valuable for us to consider both what we want and what we are willing to give up or sacrifice in order to have a complete picture of the future.

Vision is often thought of as results: we want to be worth X amount of money or have Y achievement. But again, let's put those visions aside, because those are not visions that are going to move everyone through the organization. We are talking about an organization vision, not a project vision. We are looking for a vision that people in the organization from the top to the bottom can get behind.

Perhaps the best questions we can ask are

Who do we want to become as an organization?

What will we be known for, or known as, in the community, as an organization?

What will we be proud to say our identity is in the business community when we arrive?

Business is about who we are becoming—it is a journey, not a destination. But just like the balance sheet takes a snapshot of who we are at the moment in terms of the numbers, the vision should give us a snapshot of who we are as a culture, as an organization, and as a part of the ecosystem of our industry.

What are some visions of what you see your organization looking like in the future?

Values Drill Down

Now we have a working mission and vision. Values can seem cliché; many companies have similar values. But this is not about words, it is about how we demonstrate them at the organization. If we take our attention off the words and definitions of them—and foresee the future where our behavior is aligned with the values—then what are we going to choose? What words would we *not* use to tell people about the organization? Values are the behaviors you agree to live by and align with on a daily basis when you walk through the front doors of the business. These are principles that you are going to bring to life by your example, or do everything you can to distinguish where you are not aligned with those values (in certain moments, on certain days, or in certain conversations) and how to get aligned.

Choosing the values of the organization is to say, "I believe strongly that these standards will demonstrate the most important behaviors to us as a culture." We can assume the ones we don't choose are inherent in professional environments. For example, just because we don't list "integrity" as one of our values doesn't mean that we are okay with a culture of lying people. But if integrity is a value that is core to the heart of the team—and you feel like every day you want to wake up and think about the word *integrity* and how it lives in your life, teams, and organization—then that is a word that needs to be used in the values conversation.

If you woke up every day and had certain words or phrases posted on your bathroom mirror, as a reminder about the most important things to you in life, what would those be?

Let me offer a twist in the usual way of thinking about values, instead of sorting through the endless words of Good Samaritans.

Where do you notice a lack of alignment, friction, or tension in the culture, where certain values need to be maintained consistently on an ongoing basis to create the culture you want?

Great work! You've now drafted (or at least thought about and mapped out a plan to create) your mission, vision, and values. Here are some examples from our clients:

———

Baxter Manufacturing is a leading provider of commercial ovens, bread products, proofers, and bakery specialty accessories and products. When you enjoy a crispy sandwich at Panera or a delectable treat at Dunkin' Donuts, Baxter helped make it happen.

Mission: Through our new and innovative products we empower our customers to transform how they do business.

Vision: To be recognized as the world leader in innovative oven design and technology providing unique cutting-edge solutions for the food industry markets.

Values: "ASPIRE"

A—Accountable for our actions

S—Service to our customers

P—Pride in our work

I—Innovative in our design

R—Respect toward others

E—Ethical in our behavior

———

Rising Medical Solutions is a leading medical cost containment company that serves payers of medical claims. Rising removes excessive costs, duplicate billings, inappropriate charges, and fraud from America's health-care system to keep it financially healthy for generations to come.

Mission: To protect the financial health of health care. Rising extends the availability, stability, and quality of medical care by protecting the financial health of payers, providers, and patients.

Vision: We WILL pioneer a significant breakthrough in the quality, affordability, and accessibility of health care by the year 2040.

Values:

Achieve as a Team: We embrace an open culture of learning and mentoring, where we combine our collective strengths to exceed our lofty goals.

Bushido Principles: We are guided by a code of honor, ethics, accountability, loyalty, and respect.

Create Ecstatic Customers: We cultivate devoted customer fans who are true friends and advocates of Rising.

Diamonds, Not Coal: We tirelessly strive for excellence and the extraordinary in everything we do.

Energy That Inspires: We meet challenges with an infectious enthusiasm and passion that brings out the best in others.

Foundations Foremost: We prioritize and execute our core objectives with tenacity and precision.

Laugh Often, It Is Contagious: We believe in working hard and enjoying ourselves as we do.

———

And here are the mission, vision, and values from my company, **Christine Comaford Associates**.

Mission: We believe every company culture can be high-engagement, high-performing, and foster safety, belonging, and mattering. We believe every leader can create this reality.

Vision: We are supporting the creation of one million SmartTribes by 2020.

Values: "C-I-R-C-L-E"

C—Contribution: We are here to make a difference in the world, one company culture and one leader at a time. We are known for creating rapid and lasting results.

I—Integrity: We embody what we teach, our word is our bond.

R—Reflection: We take the time to assess ourselves, our clients, and our company and make the necessary changes to foster growth.

C—Connection: We love to bring people together to help one another find resources and get what they need.

L—Learning: We are perpetual learners, always finding new and better ways to work, to grow, to improve as human beings.

E—Energy: We bring great energy to our clients, colleagues, and network because we love what we do—it is our calling in life.

Clarity of Our Intentions and Energy

Beyond clear communication is effective communication—communication that keeps everyone in their Smart State because it is concise and builds trust. Yet in the seven hundred Fortune 1000 companies and three hundred small and mid-sized companies I've worked with, I've repeatedly seen communication that is unclear and contributes to a culture of distrust.

I think it's because we're not really sure when communication is effective. There are five types of communication:

1. Information sharing
2. Requests
3. Promises
4. Sharing of oneself
5. Debating, decision making, or point proving

Yet only two drive results: requests and promises.

So if you aren't getting the results you want from an interaction with another person, the first question to ask is: "Am I making clear requests?" An example of a clear request is "Can you please get a report of our top five advertisers in the United States by revenue, renewal rate, and account manager to me by 4 P.M. Friday?" The recipient of the request understands what the request is and how to be successful in promising to fulfill it. Now they can fulfill their promise by saying "Yes, I will do that" or "No, I cannot do that, but here's what I can do . . ."

How clear is your communication? Are your requests explicit enough? Or do you have implicit intentions or expectations? Remember, unless you work for the Psychic Friends Network, you can't expect your team to know what you mean unless you tell them.

The number one place where problematic or unclear communication appears is in meetings. This is where a leader will often send people into their Critter State (by causing fear or confusion) due to lack of clarity. Why do we have meetings? Because we want to reach a conclusion of some sort. Yet typical and ineffective communication in meetings generally looks like this (see figure 4-1):

Lots of information sharing

Lots of sharing of oneself

Some debating, decision making, and point proving

Regrettably few requests and promises

Info sharing can be remarkably effective. Either information can be provided forty-eight-plus business hours prior to a meeting so that all participants arrive well informed, or it can be tightly scoped to provide the details needed to make a decision in real time. Ineffective info sharing is when a handful of people are trapped in a meeting for the sole purpose of reporting status—do that over e-mail!

Debating and decision making can be super effective when we use them without ego, when we are simply coming together to get the best decisions made at the given time with the info we have. When we have turf wars and point proving (often thinly veiled blaming) we'll rarely get the right decision, and if we do, relationships will be damaged in the process.

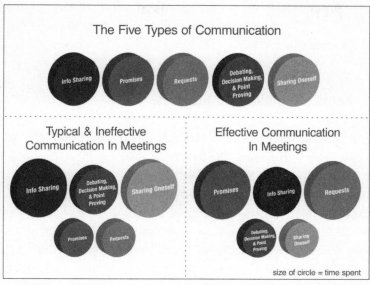

Figure 4-1. The Five Types of Communication: Only Two Drive Results

We love meetings that have an agenda—an outcome or intention—and are short, sweet, and high energy. These meetings keep everyone in their Smart State. We hate meetings that are rambling, unfocused, and send everyone into confusion—or the fight/flight/freeze of the Critter State.

So what's the difference? How can we make sure meetings matter and keep everyone in their Smart State? For starters, make sure you're using the effective communication types I mentioned above to communicate your intention with clarity. Further, your energy level will convey this by ensuring that the excitement of the words you speak is supported by the energy of your delivery (more on this in chapter 6). And last, see the Resources section below for how exactly to hold an effective meeting.

We've helped countless clients tune up their communication. The result? Meetings that are efficient and effective, and keep your team happy and clipping along to glorious accountability and execution. The key is to focus on only enough *information sharing* in order to solicit *requests* from parties who need something and *promises* from parties who will fill the need.

Increased accountability and execution are within your grasp. Do what our clients do: enlarge figure 4-1, post it on your conference room wall, and train your people to make communication more clear. The Net-Net of communication is all about promises and requests and the monitoring of both.

Stuck Spot: The Blindsided CEO

Susan came to us because her company was stuck at the $250 million inflection point. Revenue had risen to $262 million but slid back down, then hovered at $251 million for a few years, and the last year had been really scary—revenue had plunged to $207 million.

Susan was justifiably proud because the company had been featured in several magazine articles that proclaimed how wonderful and innovative the company was. She did not expect us to find anything amiss in the Cultural Assessment and quite emphatically told us so. She was certain her company's problem was not getting introduced to the right investors. But she was willing to let us do the analysis anyway so that we could help her find the real problem.

What we found shocked and depressed her. Less than 10% of the company understood the company's vision or could explain how their jobs and their performance related to it.

A bronze plaque in the lobby celebrated the company vision, and at quarterly town hall meetings a selected team member would repeat it too. Sure, they could read or even memorize the vision, but they didn't feel it. The vision didn't get them up in the morning, didn't throw fuel on their internal fire to achieve great things, didn't motivate and inspire them, and didn't stick them firmly in their Smart State.

The company's mission, vision, and values statement had been developed by The Susan (as her team called her) herself. No one else was asked to participate in the creation of the culture in a meaningful way. Oh, people sometimes got to vote on whether they wanted this or that theme for a company celebration, and the place was a well-designed, pleasant place to work, but team members seemed to feel little ownership. Because they had little involvement in shaping the world they spent ten hours per day in, inspiration was lacking. No wonder revenue was evaporating.

Deeper questioning revealed that there was little alignment in the team members' day-to-day operations and there was no sense that they were part of a team achieving anything beyond staying profitable and staying employed, when in fact the company did have some extraordinary and compelling values.

The worst part of all this was that the company was not only unable to attract new talent, it was also losing key players. The salespeople and engineers who were critical not only to the company's growth but also to the company's current level of performance were heading for the door. Without career development that was tied to the direction of the company, without a stake in continued growth, employees had little incentive to stretch above and beyond minimum performance expectations—if they chose to stay at the company at all. If this continued, the company would take an even deeper nosedive. It was time to act, and fast.

Diagnosis: The major issues all boiled down to lack of clarity. The company vision existed, but it had no impact, no emotional equity. Marketing and information technology had both lost their leaders and had no real accountability structures. The executive team was disengaged and constantly looked to Susan for guidance or intervention in internal turf wars, which led to rampant misunderstandings and divisiveness.

We hunkered down with Susan and set the ground rules. Together we would rebuild this culture. She'd be a key part of it, but when we told her to back off and let her people drive, she agreed to do so.

After ninety days of leadership training and one-on-one coaching for Susan and her executive team members, the team had gradually become more and more engaged in their Smart State and less committed to their Critter State. They began to see themselves not just as managers but as *leaders* who were responsible for communicating clearly with their energy and intention just as much as with their words and directions.

We rounded up the management team for beer and pizza late one afternoon. Together we formed a code of conduct (explicitly naming value-based behaviors) that everyone vowed to uphold. Next, we drafted the company's mission, vision, and values. Were they perfect? Nope. Did they motivate and inspire the team? Yep. That was a solid start. Even better was that the executive team insisted on emphasizing the two most effective forms of communication at this meeting: requests and promises. Once they had the hang of it and saw the results it produced, each and every one of them committed to holding their teams accountable to creating effective meetings. The company's

meeting rooms were soon plastered with our Five Types of Communication chart (again making desired cultural norms explicit) and the
new focus resulted in significantly fewer complaints about meetings.

Then we implemented new formats for communicating the company vision with clarity, and overhauled the accountability and reward
structures (see chapter 5). Within ninety more days, the executives
and all team members were supporting one another in living their
mission, vision, and values. The new statements were not that different from Susan's version, but the team owned them and they were
stated in a common language, so they could *feel* their importance.

The firm is now able to consistently attract the talent they need—
and the communication and clarity structures helped the entire team
see into their blind spots. One year later Susan's company was zoom-
ing toward $270 million in revenue (from $207 million the previous
year), with the $500 million inflection point as the target in four years
or less.

Twitter Takeaways

Find these helpful? Tweet them to your tribe and reference #SmartTribes
as the source. Thanks!

- We send team members into their Critter State and squash
  productivity, innovation, safety, belonging, and mattering if
  we don't use clear, direct communication.
- An emotionally engaging mission, vision, and values statement will help your team get connected to your company's
  cause.
- Of the five types of communication, only two move results
  forward: requests and promises. Make sure you're focusing on
  those—and training your team to do the same as well.
- Do you know your company vision? Do your team members
  know it? Do they feel emotional about it?
- Being truly clear means we need to take the time to discover
  what we need, to articulate it clearly, and to be sure the other
  party understood our communication.

- An MBA is optional but a GSD (Get Stuff Done) is essential.
- Why are we in business? Why are we doing what we do here? Why does this organization exist?
- If you woke up every day and had certain words or phrases posted on your bathroom mirror, as a reminder about the most important things to you in life, what would those be?
- Where do you notice a lack of alignment, friction, or tension in the culture, where certain values need to be maintained consistently on an ongoing basis to create the culture you want?

Assess

How direct and clear are you? Let's find out.

- Think of a scenario where you aren't getting the result you want with another person. Perhaps a direct report, colleague, friend, or family member isn't following through on expectations you have.
- Now make two columns side by side. Label the first "Explicit" (i.e., clear and direct) and the second "Implicit."
- List the explicit expectations you have of that person—these are expectations you have clearly verbalized.
- Next fill in the Implicit column—these are expectations that have not been verbalized, or things we expect someone to figure out without clearly telling them what we need or expect.
- Total up your explicit and implicit expectations. Do you have more implicit than explicit—or the opposite? Or equal?

Act

- Use the example in the Assess section above, or choose another example where you want to get better results with another person. Now meet with the person to explain this exercise and go over your implicit expectations.
- Encourage them to ask you for more clarity, and be sure to make it safe to do so. And when they do, thank them for helping you become a better leader.

ROI

We find that within a mere few weeks of receiving increased direct-
ness and clarity, a team member will feel safer and will understand
the structure they are operating within. The results are improved
relations, reduced frustration, and increased follow-through and
ownership.

Here are some of the results from our clients who have increased
their clarity:

- Individuals are 67–100% more emotionally engaged, loyal,
  accountable, and ownership-focused.
- New products and services are created 29–48% faster.
- 97% tangibly contribute to increasing key executive strategic/
  high-value time by five to fifteen hours per week.
- 100% report the ability to apply communication techniques
  and thinking styles both at home and at work and a resulting
  increase in personal fulfillment.

Resources

Helpful resources in this chapter include the following:

- The three domains of clarity
- The five types of communication

—————

Here's an exercise to help clarify where communication is breaking
down. You can do this alone or with an observer to give you additional
feedback:

1. Set up three chairs (two opposite each other and a third chair
   for the observer).
2. Think of a business challenge involving yourself and another
   person you are in conflict with.

3. Now sit in chair 1. Look at chair 2 and imagine the person is sitting there. Tell him your concerns/challenges and what you want from him.

4. Now move to chair 2. Look at chair 1 and imagine you are in the other person's brain. Now speak to "you" in chair 1. Tell yourself your concerns/challenges and what you want from "you."

5. Now sit in chair 3. Speaking to an imagined audience, explain what the challenge is between the two people in chairs 1 and 2. Speak from the standpoint of an unbiased observer.

6. The goal is to see both sides as they rotate through the experience and increase clarity of communication by understanding all sides. (This is also a powerful exercise to increase influence.)

———

Here's my *Forbes* blog post on how to hold an effective meeting: http://onforb.es/yA8Ddu.

———

Go to www.ChristineComaford.com/resources and download the kits that will be most helpful for you. We think the following kits would be a good start:

- Knowing What You Want and How to Get There: Why Are You Building This Company?
- Assess Your Team's Performance
- Optimize Your Daily Operations: Standard Operating Procedures to Streamline Your Operations

Also check out the following in the appendix:

- Values Exercise
- Energy Recall

5.

ACCOUNTABILITY
Move the Needle

A well-orchestrated team depends on everyone doing their job, at the time they are supposed to do it, yielding the results they are supposed to yield. Everyone likes to think they are accountable. Are they? As a leader, you need to ensure that your team actually is accountable.

What does accountability mean to you? Does it mean that your word is your bond? That you can be relied on to follow through? That you'll set expectations and ensure you'll honor them? Are your team members taking on too little or too much accountability? How can we be more accountable and inspire our teams to be so?

Being accountable is essential to lead, to feel influential, and to help your team feel you are worthy of trust. When we're accountable, we feel amped because we're getting high-value results, and our team feels we're transparent and trustworthy. So why is being accountable sometimes hard? Because consistently giving and keeping our word requires us to be truly considerate—of both ourselves and others. Accountability requires us to buck up and follow through even when we don't feel like it. It also requires us to value ourselves and others.

SmartTribe Accelerator #3: Accountability

To get accountability in the DNA of our developing SmartTribe, we have to build appropriate "containers." These containers are the structures that enable a group of people to achieve real accountability across the board, pulling together like a synchronized rowing team. There are four key practices that will help you do that:

1. Utilize the accountability equation.
2. Create clear accountability structures with Needle Movers.
3. Track results via weekly reporting.
4. Reward high performance and provide consequences for low performance.

Making these practices explicit keeps team members in their Smart State. They know what they have to do and how to do it. These practices not only foster safety, belonging, and mattering, they also help create two tasty brain chemicals: dopamine, which is triggered by the desire for reward; and oxytocin, which is triggered by the feeling of connection. Both are essential in fostering a SmartTribe.

1. Utilize the Accountability Equation

Most of us encourage accountability by implementing rewards and consequences as part of our culture. This is highly effective. What helps even more is if accountability is one of your core values, and so becomes ingrained and celebrated in your culture. Here's our recipe for accountability:

Assigner's Clear Expectation
+ Owner's Agreement
+ Personal Rewards and Consequences
= Self-Ownership and High Accountability

Accountability starts at the top, and this is where many companies struggle.

When the leader takes responsibility for unspoken expectations, team members will fall right into line to mirror their boss. The flip side is true too—in low-accountability cultures, we see that the trouble begins at the top. The team is simply modeling the low accountability that the executive team is displaying.

Do you have an accountability partner? This is a person you check in with weekly to share what you accomplished, what you didn't and why, and what you'll accomplish in the coming week. He or she should be a peer and ideally in a different division or department in order to provide an unbiased perspective. An accountability partner is also a terrific sounding board to help you stay focused on your Needle Movers (more on this below) as well as your high-value activities (more on this in chapter 8). I speak with mine via phone each Friday afternoon. We both e-mail our weekly status to each other in advance.

What consequences do you set for yourself and your team when accountability is dropped? Consequences remind us that not keeping our commitments will carry repercussions. Most of us were raised with consequences ("If you don't finish your dinner, you won't get dessert"; "If you don't get good grades, you won't get into college"), so I find we can foster safety, belonging, and mattering by setting and upholding consequences.

With consequences we're safe, because we know that if we don't hand in our weekly hours, for example, we won't get paid. That's how it works here. We all have the same consequences; we're a team; we belong together. It matters if I perform—I see how I make a difference here. Likewise, it matters if I don't perform—I am letting the team down.

2. Create Clear Accountability Structures with Needle Movers

Now let's talk about some successful accountability structures and look at some examples.

I find that many people struggle with overwhelm and lack of focus because they aren't defining their Needle Movers and exclusively working on them.

We all need help identifying the key activities to focus on right now that *move the needle*—those activities that move your business forward from zero to ten miles per hour, or from ten to fifty miles per hour, or from fifty to one hundred miles per hour. Distilling your business to its essence is key here. Maybe to move your business forward you need to generate more sales leads, close more sales, or train your team to be self-managed. At any given time, everyone on your team should focus on and report on their own Needle Movers. I encourage you to distill your Needle Movers to only three, because each of these three activities will have subactivities beneath them, and three key priorities are plenty to focus on.

I prefer the term "Needle Mover" as opposed to "goal." Goals are binary—you achieve them and feel great, or you don't and feel lousy. You won't always achieve the exact result you want. This doesn't mean you have failed! A result is a result, and it will move your business forward.

A Needle Mover is a given result that will have a significant impact on the success of your business. Once you determine your Needle Movers and create and follow a plan to achieve them, you'll see daily, weekly, monthly, quarterly, and annual results. Tangible results keep you excited; they build and maintain your momentum.

Set a Target ("T" in table 5-1 below), Minimum (Min), and Mind Blower (MB) for each Needle Mover. The Target is what you want, the Minimum is the worst case you are willing to accept, and the Mind Blower is what would absolutely rock your world. If you want to simplify, set Targets and Mind Blowers only.

Your annual Needle Movers will be supported by your monthly and quarterly ones.

As you start to drill down on your Needle Movers, you'll see how to distribute the work over the coming months and across your various team members.

Stuck Spot: Vague Outcomes

Stan, the CEO of a home-wares business, brought us in because his business had been stuck between the $50 million and $100 million inflection points for three years. He was getting bored with the business and felt disillusioned. He felt stuck, overworked, overly accountable, and unsure about how to get out of this state.

It quickly became apparent to Stan that he had a major accountability issue—not only was the team not being held accountable but

Stan himself had drifted into a lackadaisical attitude toward his own future.

Diagnosis: Pervasive low accountability, starting at the top.

Our first initiative with Stan was to set his Needle Movers—specific outcomes we could drive toward together. Let's walk through the process.

Stan's Needle Movers:

1. $85 million in revenue (Target: $85 million, Minimum: $82 million, Mind Blower: $90 million+)
2. Weekends off (Target: 75% off, Minimum: 50% off, Mind Blower: *all* weekends off for the year)
3. Cut costs by 20% (Target: 20%, Minimum: 15%, Mind Blower: 25%+)

Now he must drill down on how exactly he will achieve these Needle Movers. Otherwise he might as well just set goals—which often are simply vague, unaccountable *desires*.

Here are Stan's drill-downs on his annual Needle Movers:

1. For $85 million in revenue: Train his existing salespeople in neuroscience-based influencing techniques (see chapters 6–7 for more on these techniques) to close more sales and close faster, add fifteen or more new retail channels, increase online sales by 20% or more, recruit five new salespeople, forge alliances with ten or more companies with complementary products for bidirectional web sales and promotions, and attend five or more trade shows.

First he may want to recruit five new salespeople and get everyone trained in neuroscience-based influencing techniques, *so* he can add fifteen or more new retail channels, and *then* forge alliances with ten or more companies with complementary products for bidirectional web sales and promotion. *In parallel*, his team will attend five or more trade shows, *which will lead to* increasing online sales by 20% or more through the year. And yes—he needs to quantify what amount of revenue he wants from his various channels: online sales, alliances, direct sales, and phone sales.

This month's first step: Start process to recruit five new salespeople and get everyone trained in neuroscience-based influencing techniques.

2. For weekends off: Delegate more to his COO, get his executive team leadership training and coaching, help set Needle Movers for each executive team member, and determine what he can defer or ditch entirely.

First he'll want to rank his high-value activities (things he is great at and that make a huge difference to the company's growth) and low-value activities (things he is not great at and can easily delegate). *Then* he'll decide what to delegate, defer until later, or ultimately ditch and not do at all. *Next* he'll get his team leadership training and coaching so they can support him in releasing his micromanaging tendencies (hooray!). *In parallel,* he'll delegate all he can to his COO and other executive team members. *Then* he'll host a Needle Mover training and scoping session so his team will understand what needs to be achieved by when, how it will be achieved, and who will own it. *And following this* he'll work with us on an updated incentive plan so rewards and consequences will be clear and compelling. Phew!

This month's first step: Rank high-value activities (things he is great at and that make a huge difference to the company's growth) and low-value activities (things he is not great at and can easily delegate).

3. To cut costs by 20%: Task finance to work out new terms with his existing manufacturing sources or find new ones, task operations to streamline internal processes, task sales and client care to implement service-level agreements so the excessive free client service ends, and implement the use of standard operating procedures (SOPs) across all departments.

First he'll get finance working on new terms with existing manufacturing sources or finding new ones. *In parallel,* he'll task operations with examining their top three to five most burdensome processes, so they can create and implement SOPs in their department and model SOP use for the other departments (see more on SOPs below). *This will lead to* client care reviewing client contracts and service load to assess what service-level agreements would make sense to offer. *Then* client care can loop in sales and finance to share their findings and set pricing and communication strategies for the new service-level agreements.

This month's first step: Get finance working on setting new terms with existing manufacturing sources or finding new manufacturing sources.

You'll notice that in the above scenario many of Stan's Needle Movers had to be done by someone else. Guess how he was going to hold them accountable. You got it: with the accountability equation and explicit requests and promises (remember clarity from chapter 4?).

The next time you're overwhelmed or lack of focus creeps up, count on your Needle Movers to shed light on where your energy and time should be allocated. As a result you'll see a significant increase in your own productivity and focus, as well as that of your team, because you'll reduce Critter State triggering.

3. Track Results via Weekly Reporting

A key aspect of accountability is visibility: knowing what your key team members are doing each week to avoid surprises or missed results.

Here's an example of a weekly reporting template we used with Bill, Stan's VP of sales. Note that the two examples below show plans for the beginning of the month of October, with the results of the previous month (September) in the fifth column.

Bill is responsible for U.S. sales only. His annual Needle Movers are tied to increasing overall revenue, increasing gross margin, and increasing field sales rep revenue. Their reps are independent contractors on a pay-for-performance compensation plan, so every dollar in sales from them has a much higher margin than sales from the internal direct salespeople.

Notice that Bill was tracking Target (T), Minimum (Min), and Mind Blower (MB) for his annual Needle Movers too. Here's where he stood at the beginning of October:

TABLE 5-1. NEEDLE MOVER WEEKLY REPORTING FOR VP OF SALES: FIRST WEEK OF OCTOBER	
Completed Week of 10/01 + Weekly Win	Design retailer sales kit.
	Meet with development to consolidate product lines.
	Meet with finance re: reducing collection times by 20%.
	Strategic planning off site.
	4 client meetings re: 2013 orders.
	Weekly Win: 4 new reps onboarded!

Key Projects: Week of 10/08	Meet with client care to design client service rep upsell/downsell/cross-sell scripts.
	Meet with inventory team to set fill rates, turn, and aging rates for 2013.
	Train new account manager in sales process.
	5 client meetings re: 2013 orders
October Needle Mover Status	*Monthly revenue: Current $2.1 million* T: $7 million, Min: $6 million, MB: $7.5 million+
	Monthly gross margin: Current 7.1% T: 8%, Min: 6.5%, MB: 10%
	2013 rep quotas, sales process, training dates set: TBD T: 10/22, Min: 10/29, MB: 10/15
Annual Needle Mover Status	*Revenue: Current $63.77 million* T: $85 million, Min: $82 million, MB: $90 million+
	Gross margin: Current 7.5% T: 8%, Min: 6.5%, MB: 10%
	% revenue from rep channel: Current 41% T: 45%, Min: 40%, MB: 50%+
Previous Month Results	*Monthly revenue: $7.17 million* T: $7 million, Min: $6 million, MB: $7.5 million
	Monthly gross margin: 7.5% T: 8%, Min: 6.5%, MB: 10%
	New strategic accounts: 4 T: 4, Min: 3, MB: 5

TABLE 5-2. NEEDLE MOVER WEEKLY REPORTING FOR VP OF SALES: FIRST WEEK OF NOVEMBER	
Completed Week of 11/05 + Weekly Win	Approved final retailer sales kit.
	4 client meetings re: 2013 orders.
	Finished client service rep upsell/downsell/cross-sell scripts.
	Finished client service rep, rep, retailer sales SOPs.
	Weekly Win: 4 new reps onboarded.
Key Projects: Week of 11/12	Train 10 retailers in sales kit.
	Set client service rep quotas with client care.
	Design monthly communication to reps, client service reps, retailers, key accounts with marketing.
	Finalize 2013 marketing promo plan.
	2 client meetings re: 2013 orders.

(continued on next page)

(continued from previous page)

TABLE 5-2. NEEDLE MOVER WEEKLY REPORTING FOR VP OF SALES: FIRST WEEK OF NOVEMBER	
November Needle Mover Status *(Note changes to bolded items due to October's performance)*	***Monthly revenue: Current $3.5*** T: $8 million, Min: $7.5 million, MB: $8.5 million ***Monthly gross margin: Current 7.7%*** T: 8.25%, Min: 7.5%, MB: 10% ***2013 CSR quotas, sales process, training dates set: TBD*** T: 11/12, Min: 11/19, MB: 11/5
Annual Needle Mover Status	*Revenue: Current $72.67 million* T: $85 million, Min: $82 million, MB: $90 million+ *Gross margin: Current 7.5%* T: 8%, Min: 6.5%, MB: 10% *% revenue from rep channel: Current 42%* T: 45%, Min: 40%, MB: 50%+
Previous Month Results	*Monthly revenue: $7.5 million* T: $7 million, Min: $6 million, MB: $7.5 million+ *Monthly gross margin: 7.8%* T: 8%, Min: 6.5%, MB: 10% *2013 rep quotas, sales process, training dates set: 10/26* T: 10/20, Min: 10/29, MB: 10/15

Because he is now tracking his monthly results, you'll see from the bold items above that Bill has increased his revenue and gross margin Targets, Minimums, and Mind Blowers. Note that it took only ninety days for him to realize that he could be performing at a higher level than he had expected. Interesting, yes? Often we and our team members perform at levels lower than we are able to simply because of an absence of Needle Movers and results tracking. Once Stan and his team set and tracked their Needle Movers, they reached the $100 million revenue inflection point in eighteen months. Now they have $250 million in their sights. It all comes down to accountability.

One of Stan's tasks to complete his Needle Mover of cutting costs by 20% was to create and implement SOPs. Does your company have clear SOPs? SOPs are crucial for both clarity and accountability. If you don't have clear processes for getting things done, all kinds of things can run amok—you'll get inconsistent work processes, inconsistent quality, and inconsistent outcomes.

Before our team started developing SOPs for our key tasks, we often had communication gaps. It would make me crazy when someone would say, "But I didn't know I was supposed to do X!"

After much discussion and reflection, I realized I was the culprit—I would give the key directions explicitly, and then I'd expect the team member to fill in the blanks (uh-oh—implicit expectations), which seemed obvious to me. Yet the blanks were often the most crucial parts of the task or project. SOPs keep us honest. Seriously. It's easy to drop key communication nuggets without them. If you don't have them, creating and implementing SOPs are likely a key component of one or more of your Needle Movers.

See the Resources section of this chapter for help creating accountability structures and SOPs.

4. Reward High Performance and Provide Consequences for Low Performance

Incentive plans are highly customized to a company culture and a team member's specific role. But no matter what your specific incentive plan is, the point is we create more emotional engagement, more excitement, and anticipation of treats when we spell out what exceptional, adequate, and poor performance will net a person.

And if you don't have cash to reward high performance, it's not the end of the world. Social rewards are far more powerful anyway, and besides, compensation can be in points (that are then quarterly or annually turned in for a day off, a massage, a prepaid credit or gift card, a higher percentage of the bonus pool available for colleagues of your category, etc.). The main point is to have rewards and consequences for the company, the team, and the individual to keep everyone in their Smart State.

If the company exceeds their Needle Movers, there is a celebration and everyone prospers. If the team does as well—again, celebration and prospering. If the individual rises up to peak performance, he or she will be celebrated and prosper. Recognition is one of the best rewards, which is why in addition to having an incentive plan you'll want to create something like our clients do with their Rock Star of the Month program, Shout Outs, and more. See chapter 11 to learn how.

Consequences That Work

Let's consider consequences for a minute. For one of our clients, if you don't send in your weekly status by Monday at 7 A.M., you are not permitted to attend the management team meeting at 8 a.m. They hold this firm—heck, if managers aren't getting their status in on time, what sort of message are they sending to their reports? Other consequences (beyond the most drastic of demotion or termination) include withholding privileges when performance is poor. I like to keep things simple on the consequences front, because if you hire people who are aligned with your values, and you have a clear culture of performance and accountability, consequences will need to be applied only rarely. We use the four steps below. Then, if a team member continues to struggle, we set a thirty-, sixty-, or ninety-day counseling/correction period (whatever you choose to call it). If that doesn't work, we help transition the employee out of the company.

Here are standard consequences we've found to work very well when a team member doesn't keep commitments:

- First miss: Ask, "Are you okay?" Maybe your team member is dealing with a personal life disaster, and his life has been turned upside down. If he answers yes, then remind him how essential accountability is to the culture and to your trusting him—and walk him through setting up calendar reminders if need be. If he answers no, and he is not okay, work with him as best you can to help him through this personal crisis. Lightening his workload may be required.
- Second miss: Ask, "Do you have too much work?" If so, help lighten his workload. If not, stress how crucial accountability is to trust and ask how he will ensure he's accountable in the future.
- Third miss: Ask, "Is your role too big?" It appears that his role is too demanding for his ability. It may now be time to discuss if he is in the right role and if he needs to move to a reduced role, shift to flex time, or some other option to ensure you get the performance he had promised. At this stage you'll want to bring Human Resources into the conversation.
- Fourth miss: Ask, "Do you really want to work here?" His behavior is showing that he doesn't. That's okay. Just have a frank conversation about the situation so that everyone's

needs can be met. If he insists he wants to stay at the company and in his current role, then design a counseling period where he'll demonstrate and maintain improved performance starting immediately. If the counseling period concludes and his performance isn't improved, it's time for a transition.

If you want to know what a person is truly committed to, look at their calendar, their credit card statement, and their behavior. These will reveal their priorities and what they value most.

How Trust Is Broken and Egos Are Triggered

Accountability is so deeply tied to promises and trust that safety, belonging, and mattering are quickly damaged when accountability is dropped. As leaders, it's key when administering consequences to determine if accountability is being dropped because the person is in their Critter State and is stuck, or if she is intentionally uncooperative.

In my experience, trust is broken in three levels:

- Capability: Is the person truly capable of doing what was promised? Capability breaches of trust are the easiest to fix. We either help her get the skill she needs or move her to a new role.
- Commitment: Is she committed to following through on what was promised? Commitment breaches are more tricky—when a person repeatedly drops commitments we must find out what the underlying cause is. Use an Outcome Frame to achieve this. Ask her, "What do you want? What will having that do for you? When will you know when you have it?" Once this is clear, we can help her shift to keeping commitments. See more on Outcome Frames in chapter 6.
- Character: If a person keeps making promises and breaking them, who is she, really? She doesn't seem to have a consistent character we can count on. Character breaches are the hardest, since we now doubt who the person really is. Was it all a front? Who's behind the mask? Breaches of this type can take years of demonstrating consistency to win back trust.

Now let's talk about how the ego is triggered and how we unintentionally send someone into their Critter State. This happens when we question someone's

- Competence (sounds like safety, yes?): If you openly question someone's ability, you are poking at the ego's cage, so don't be surprised to hear a roar. Better to discover their level of competence and help them increase it.
- Significance (sounds like mattering, doesn't it?): If you talk down to a person and see them as beneath you, be ready for the ego to attack—which could be in a passive-aggressive sabotaging manner.
- Lovability (this triggers safety, belonging, and mattering issues): Leaders often suggest lovability isn't questioned in business scenarios. Not so! There are always team members who are perceived as "above the law" or in the "in crowd"— that is, more lovable. Those on the outside can damage your culture through dissent. Better to love all.

On the flip side, as we reinforce and celebrate someone's competence, appreciate their contributions and significance, and foster a culture of equality and transparency (thus lovability), we'll help our team stay in their Smart State.

Now that you know how trust is broken and egos are triggered, in the next chapter we'll work on rebuilding and confirming trust and keeping ego reactions in check.

▼

Twitter Takeaways

Find these helpful? Tweet them to your tribe and reference #SmartTribes as the source. Thanks!

- Accountability works with structures to support it: Needle Movers, tracking (weekly reporting), and incentives (rewards and consequences).

- When accountability structures are used across a company, you'll find people that perform at much higher levels. If a bar isn't set, people don't know how high they can jump.
- Success with accountability requires that we help provide structures and containers so our team can stay in their Smart State. Trust and ego flare-ups put us in our Critter State.
- What does accountability mean to you? Does it mean that your word is your bond? That you can be relied on to follow through?
- Assigner's Clear Expectation + Owner's Agreement + Personal Rewards and Consequences = Self-Ownership and High Accountability
- What consequences do you set for yourself and your team when accountability is dropped? Consequences remind us that not keeping our commitments will carry repercussions.
- If you want to know what a person is truly committed to, look at their calendar, their credit card statement, and their behavior. These will reveal their priorities and what they value most.
- Trust is broken in three levels: capability, commitment, character. The ego is triggered by questioning someone's significance, competence, lovability.

Assess

Answer the following questions to assess your company's level of accountability. Do you

1. Utilize the accountability equation?
2. Create clear accountability structures?
3. Track results with weekly reporting?
4. Have rewards for high performance and consequences for low performance?

Act

- Based on your answers above, where could your accountability be strengthened?

- Create a ninety-day plan to design and deploy structures for the gaps in your accountability. If your challenge is company-wide, you may find that a cross-functional accountability task force will yield buy-in and results faster.
- See our Resources section for templates, and call us if you need help.

ROI

Our clients find that when they apply the four practices above they see tremendous ROI within as little as six months. You will need talent (that's what we call human resources) to help you implement and manage the above.

- Individuals become 35–50% more productive.
- 97% tangibly contribute to increasing key executive strategic/high-value time by five to fifteen hours per week.
- 63% receive a promotion to a role with increased responsibility and management of others within six months of receiving coaching in accountability and leadership.
- 86% report getting more done in less time due to the accountability techniques they learned.

Resources

Helpful resources in this chapter include the following:

- Accountability equation
- Weekly reporting
- Rewards and consequences

Go to www.ChristineComaford.com/resources and download the kits that will be most helpful for you. We think the following kits would be a good start:

- Increasing Accountability and Ensuring Goals Are Met
- Optimize Your Daily Operations: Standard Operating Procedures to Streamline Your Operations
- Streamlining Your Sales Funnel
- Marketing Optimization and Focus
- Assess Your Team's Performance

Also check out the following in the appendix:

- Needle Mover Worksheet

6.

INFLUENCE
Load the Dice

J ust about every CEO, every executive, and every manager with
whom we work wants to be more influential. The neuroscience
techniques in this and the next chapter provide simple and
profound ways of increasing influence by increasing safety, belonging,
and mattering. These practices will help you manage better, sell
better, and speak with stakeholders better. They'll even improve your
personal life.

But there's a catch. Stepping up to be a leader isn't about getting
anything for yourself. It's about service. The more influential you become, the more you are putting yourself at the service of your team.

Real influence is about empowering others.

The influencing tools we describe below serve to foster team coop-
eration, keep people in their Smart State, and nurture a SmartTribe.
These tools work at the level of your subconscious mind, which is
where 90% of your behaviors come from, according to the Hoffman
Institute. They help you shift your most challenging emotions, since
90% of our reactions are emotional, and our emotions respond four
hundred times faster than our intellect.[1] And as a leader how you come
across emotionally is essential, since 50–70% of the entire emotional
state of an organization is set by the leaders.[2]

SmartTribe Accelerator #4: Influence

Here's the thing about influence: it's not about how many people you can tell what to do. It's about how many people you can understand, empower, and motivate. So the key to developing influence is developing your ability to build rapport, or connect, with anyone. And the key to developing rapport is flexibility of behavior and the desire to step into someone else's world. When we are influential we feel flexible and powerful, and our team feels that we're capable and collaborative.

Have you ever had the experience of watching someone you care about dive into self-defeating behavior? You can see so clearly what needs to shift, but it seems like the more you say or do to try to help, the less effect you have. Why? The person does not feel safe enough to hear you.

Essentially rapport is that state of connection where our critter brain is peering out and coding who is a friend and who is a foe. A person in this state is determining who is "similar to me" and thus safe. The critter brain is responsible for survival and is constantly scanning for threats. Imagine we're antelopes out on the savanna. The critter brain is relaxed because it has scanned the environment and decided it's with other antelopes and not with lions. Rapport is rampant, in terms of how the critter brain is calculating safety ("Yep, only us antelopes out here"). Once we've established a feeling of safety and have access to the prefrontal cortex, we're in our Smart State and capable of making plans and initiating positive changes.

In order to change or shift or accept feedback there has to be a pre-existent condition of rapport with the critter—or the brain will be too busy ensuring its survival to accept any other solution, no matter how elegant, right, logical, or plain old commonsensical it may seem to the rest of us. Survival—meaning continued breathing—always trumps any other impulse.

Just Another Antelope?

To be coded as "just another antelope," the brain must see you as "similar to me." So to create rapport we "mirror" the person with whom we are present. Mirroring is primal. It goes in straight to our safety parts and lets them say "aaaahhhh." Try making a funny face at a baby. Most babies will imitate it right back at you. When you mirror their facial expressions they often gurgle and smile back at you, as if to say "I get it, I'm here and loved and safe!" Many mothers automatically have these kinds of interactions with their children. It's instinctual.

To see natural rapport in action just go to any restaurant and watch some couples. You can tell the current state of any of the relationships by how much unconscious mirroring is going on. Happy couples are a connected unit with mirroring and rapport in their body language, and unhappy couples are out of sync in their body language and have low mirroring. Sometimes the rapport is palpable from across the room. You see the same thing with friends, and it is particularly noticeable with groups of teens. As they explore their own identities as different from their parents', they imitate one another's hand gestures, clothing, facial expressions, and lingo in order to feel a sense of belonging.

Adult mirroring can be full body (i.e., adopting the same body position), feedback of key gestures or words, auditory (matching tone, volume, or speed of speaking), breathing, or kinesthetic (matching energy dynamics). Effective mirroring can help shift unstable states like anger, depression, or anxiety by first matching (pacing) and then gradually shifting (leading) to a more calm state. If real rapport—safety—has been established first, you can help lead someone to a different state. Without rapport their system will most likely go into a defensive stance and resist matching you.

Have you ever seen a child have a fit in a supermarket? Most of the time, the parent starts speaking to the child in a soft tone, trying to encourage him or her to calm down. And most of the time that approach doesn't work—and if it does, it's usually because of a whispered threat. Awhile back I saw a terrific ad[3] with a mother using rapport. A mom and her child are in a supermarket and the child is grabbing bags of treats. The mother shakes her head, the child has a fit, the mother matches the child's fit, and immediately the child stops, stunned. What happened? The mother stepped into the child's world and he suddenly realized they were the same. His game wouldn't work with her. As one of our clients says, sometimes people put the "right em-PHA-sis on the wrong syl-LA-ble."

Manipulation—or Stepping onto Someone's Map?

When we teach rapport, we often get a question about manipulation. It goes something like this: "Isn't that kind of slimy? If you mirror and match, aren't you being manipulative?" The answer is directly related to your intention. Are you using these techniques to respectfully understand another's Map, to create safety? Once you have rapport, are you going to use it to empower others, building everyone's influence? Or are you going to use it only to further your own self-interest with command and control?

When you build rapport with other people, you necessarily understand them better. You can't help but step onto their Map of the world. You see, none of us sees the world in exactly the same way. Instead, we each have a Map of the world that's based on our perceptions and experiences. Our Map houses our beliefs, shapes our identity, and determines our behavior, both the things we want to do and our responses to what happens to us. Everyone's Map is unique, and without it we'd be lost, with no clue who to be and how to function in the world. We'll explain the aspects of a person's Map more deeply in chapter 9 where we cover Logical Levels of Change.

Figure 6-1. Your Map of the World

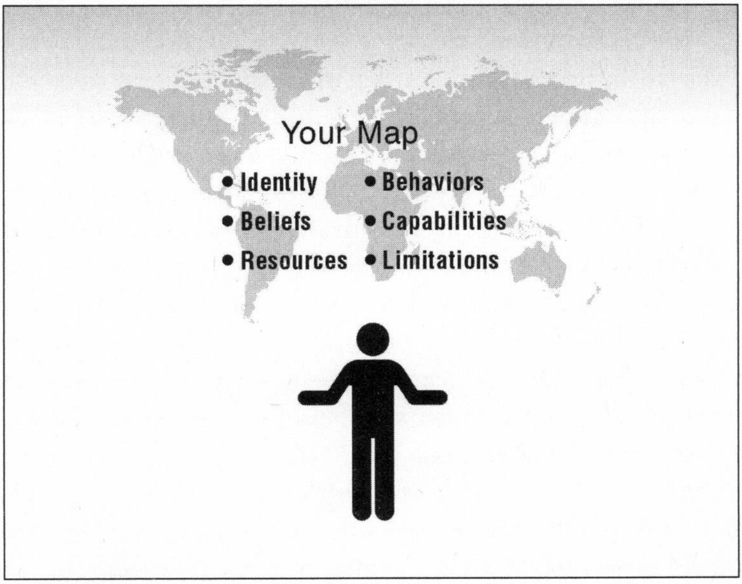

Your Map

- Identity
- Behaviors
- Beliefs
- Capabilities
- Resources
- Limitations

The Map Is the Territory

You can edit or enhance Maps—our own and other people's—by creating access to useful resources, recoding resources, and reframing or adding new understandings. Very few people know how to do this effectively because it's deeply ingrained in the subconscious mind. This is one reason you're reading this book—to learn the potent neuroscience techniques to edit your and other people's Maps.

The result of editing or enhancing someone's Map is the end, or at least the dramatic reduction, of challenging behaviors, limiting beliefs, and emotional disengagement. The business result is increased accountability, proactivity, commitment, and performance.

Maybe you have the traits of patience, compassion, and confidence on your Map—or maybe you don't and would like to. Or maybe you have access to those resources when you are with a dog or a child but not when you are with a team member. Maybe you see yourself as a person who can overcome any obstacle and see the world as a friendly place. Maybe you get easily discouraged and would like to be more resilient. These are all aspects of your identity, beliefs, limitations, behaviors, resources, and capabilities.

Whatever you're looking for, learning to change your Map will put more choice and power in your life.

- If you know how to step into other people's Maps, you'll be able to improve their abilities, performance, and outcomes, and increase their feelings of safety, belonging, trust, and connection within your team. You can use these techniques regardless of where you are in your organization: boss to subordinate, subordinate to boss, it doesn't matter. This knowledge can have a huge impact on your relationships with everyone—coworkers, subordinates, bosses, and even your spouse and children.
- Learning to edit their own and their teams' Maps is one of the reasons our clients often say they now can do and be what they never could have imagined before.

Your ecology is all the reasons you are the way you are, including the intended positive outcome of your Critter State wiring. Your ecol-

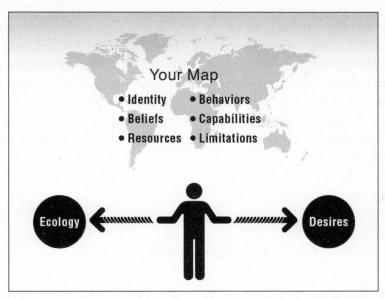

Figure 6-2. Your Map: Ecology and Desires Tug of War

ogy formed your initial Map. Your desires are simply what you want to create in your life. Now, here's the tricky part: you are stuck in the middle of a massive tug of war within your subconscious mind, being pulled in opposite directions. Equal and opposing forces are pulling you back to your ecology and pulling you forward to your desires. No wonder it can be hard to get what you want or, once you have it, to feel satisfied. In order to lessen the pull of your ecology and thus more easily fulfill your desires, you need to edit and enhance your Map—or shift how you are seeing the world.

For example, a woman I once worked with, we'll call her Janine, craved appreciation. This desire of hers fiercely conflicted with her ecology—where she was unable to actually accept appreciation. When I sent her e-mails thanking her for great work, she'd never respond. When I appreciated her in person, her face would go blank—as if she couldn't process the information I was giving her. Through inquiring about her history around appreciation she said (no surprise) that her family had no context for appreciation. People in her family just didn't praise one another.

We got to work editing her Map so she could loosen the pull of her ecology by adding the resource of appreciating herself and others. We did this via executive coaching and some of our favorite neuroscience techniques, cleared her experience of family coldness, and modeled the appreciation behavior of some of Janine's friends. Within three months Janine was giving and receiving deep levels of appreciation.

How do you enhance your Map and the Maps of others? First, you have to know what is on your Map—and perhaps what is not on it. To understand people's Maps and to make a person aware of their own Map, we use a deceptively simple series of questions known as the Outcome Frame, followed by the appropriate neuroscience process to access your subconscious mind. The Outcome Frame you can do on your own; the neuroscience process your (properly trained) executive coach can do for you.

Stuck Spot: When Success Isn't Safe

George is the CEO of a financial services company that has been barely hovering above the $25 million inflection point for five years. He wants to double his company's revenue this year. He's been stating this very achievable goal for the past three years and still hasn't reached it. Why?

When we first assessed George's behavior, he seemed to be present to his situation and his vision was clear. There were some accountability problems evident since he hadn't met his goal, but this issue was certainly not pervasive within the company. Nor was he vague about his Needle Movers or unaccountable to his team.

Diagnosis: It was not ecologically safe for him to achieve his desired outcome. The subconscious tug of war between his desires and his ecology was preventing him from getting what he wanted.

Be Present with the Present

Let's find out why George wasn't getting the doubled revenue he wanted. Here's what we learned when we worked through a basic Outcome Frame with him:

- What would you like? *To double revenue this year.*
- What will having that do for you? *I'll feel secure, be happy, have peace of mind, have less stress and a cash cushion, feel confident that*

we got to the next level and the business is scalable, work less, and know my team can step up. [What he really wanted was to feel safe—to let go of control and know it would be okay.]

- How will you know when you have it (specifically)? *Doubled revenue from last year.*

- So there you are in the future and you have what you want. What risk might you take to ensure this change is going to happen? *I might have to let go of some control—delegate more, promote some high performers and let a few low performers go, let my VP of sales run with our plan, stop micromanaging our VP of operations.* [Here comes the good stuff!]

- What will likely happen if you don't solve this the way you want? What will be the impact on your business and life? *We'll be stuck in the same rut we've been in for three years, we won't be able to grow the business and sell it for the $90 million+ that we want to, my family members and I won't get to cash out, and we'll one day have to wind the business down—without securing our and our children's financial futures.*

- What might someone have to believe about the world/company/situation to get this? *That this is possible, that they have the team to achieve this outcome, that more clients want what we have, that we can find these clients.*

- What might you have to believe about yourself? *That I can let go and things won't fall apart, that my team wants to rise up.*

- What can you appreciate about the current situation prior to change? (What's great about holding on to control?) *I know what the outcome will be—even if it isn't what I want, I trust myself and don't have to rely on others.*

From this process George realized that his key issue was fear of letting go of control, yet he would have to do this (to a degree) in order to let his team help him double revenue. But knowing this intellectually wasn't enough; in the thick of battle George would still default to controlling behavior, because it was rooted in his subconscious mind. So we needed to change this.

• • •

Then Change the Past

After we completed the Outcome Frame, it was time to excavate. When did George's controlling behavior begin? Why was relying on others so threatening? We would find out by asking the following:

- Can you recall a time when you didn't feel you had to control things?
- Was there a major life trauma when your level of controlling increased?
- Is there a trigger event you experience regularly when your controlling kicks into high gear?

The life trauma was the answer. When his parents divorced, George was seven years old. He then became the man of the house, and his father all but disappeared. Little George decided then that he would never be at the mercy of others, and such a life-altering experience, again. He'd shape his world and keep it tightly in check.

Except that strategy no longer worked for him.

So he asked me to help him change it. Using a process called Three Place Dissociation I guided George through observing this childhood trauma from a distance and then defusing the beliefs he formed then. We helped him edit his identity and belief system, which is one of the deepest levels of change we can make. This was essential in order to help him change his capabilities and behavior as a leader of his company.

We continued coaching George and began working with his executive team to shift too. The executive team had supported the command-and-control culture that George had created—they were now part of the system that everyone wanted to change.

. . . Which Changes the Future

Fast-forward nine months. George is nearing his fiscal year end. Revenue will double this year, wrapping up at a healthy $51 million. What's next? We're going to double the bottom line and increase the asset base in our continuing plan to strengthen George's company for acquisition. I'd like to see him get $145 million+ for his company instead of his $90 million goal.

Isn't it fascinating that our company and its performance are directly tied to who we are and what behaviors limit us? We self-sabotage and don't even know it! The key is to root out the true reason we aren't getting what we want and clear it. Neuroscience techniques are the fastest way to do this. The more Maps I travel on, the more compassionate I become. The more compassionate I become, the better I am at leading myself and others, and helping them get in their Smart States.

If you would like more influence by understanding and even editing your own and other people's Maps, the following three tools will help you: **rapport**, **flexible behavior**, and **influencing phrases**.

The Ultimate Precondition for Influence: Rapport

The first tool you'll need to increase influence is rapport. Building rapport is what makes our critter brain feel safe enough to make our unconscious patterning available to our conscious decision making. None of the above questioning is possible without rapport.

Chances are, you're already unconsciously doing a lot of rapport-building practices naturally (see figure 6-3).

Physical Body. This is about mirroring posture and full body position. For example, if you're in a meeting with a person who is leaning back and has his arms crossed, you adopt this posture too. If he's leaning forward, you do the same. When you do this kind of mirroring you're subtly letting the other person know that you're similar, that you've got things in common. The tricky part is to do it authentically. If you're able to tap into what he or she is feeling, you'll find that posture and gesture mirroring is surprisingly easy.

Vocal Analog. This is matching someone's tone, pace, pitch, volume, phrasing, and breathing. It sounds easy, but it's hard to pull this off and still come across as authentic. If someone sounds like Betty Boop or has a foreign accent, for example, trying to match her tone would sound bizarre and inappropriate. But matching volume, pace, phrasing, and breathing is a lot more effective.

Key Words and Gestures. This is also something we often do naturally. I'm sure you've been in a conversation where the person you were talking with used a common phrase like "We've got to go the

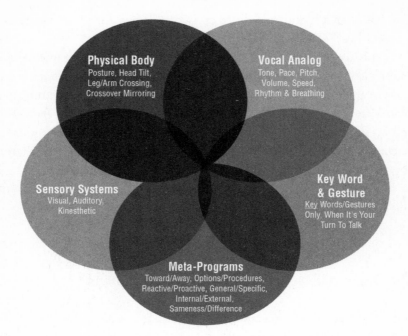

Figure 6-3. Rapport-Building Techniques

extra mile." I'm betting that within a few seconds you found yourself using that same phrase or something very similar. What you were doing was subconsciously showing the other person that you agreed, you understood, and they were safe with you.

Sensory Systems. This is the primary sense that a person uses to access the world. The three most common sensory systems are visual, kinesthetic (touch), and auditory (hearing). Yes, we all have five senses, but although gustatory (taste) and olfactory (scent) can bring up powerful memories and emotions, they're rarely as important in our day-to-day life as the other three—at least for Americans.

How can you tell someone's predominant sense? First, listen to the words and phrases she chooses. If she often talks about "long-term vision" and frequently says, "I see where you're going," there's a good chance her primary sensory system is visual. If she talks about needing to "get my arms around this" or frequently touches you, her primary sensory system is probably kinesthetic. If she asks, "Does that resonate with you?" or frequently says, "I hear what you are saying," then auditory is her primary sensory system. (And, of course, phrases like "Something smells fishy" or "That leaves a bitter taste in my mouth" could indicate a dominant olfactory or gustatory system.) Listen carefully, though. Many of us mix sensory systems in our communication.

Your job, then, to create rapport is to use words indicating the same kinds of sensory systems.

Meta Programs. This is advanced influence and rapport. It's so essential we've dedicated the entire next chapter to it.

How Flexible Is Your Behavior?

The next tool you'll need to be more influential is flexible behavior. Most of us are highly predictable. We react in predictable ways, we have predictable patterns of behavior, we have predictable speech patterns . . . we have our Maps and we're sticking to them. No wonder it's so easy for people to peg us.

There's hope. The following behavioral stances can be mixed and matched for maximum influence, maximum rapport, and maximum outcome. When we use different stances in different scenarios, we get different results.[4]

There's the

- **Mommy:** Supports the recipient fully, sees and acknowledges how great they are. As a result the recipient feels *huge*.
- **Anthropologist:** Behaves with major curiosity and high inquiry. This stance asks lots of questions and is continually curious, at times even fascinated.
- **Drill Sergeant:** Hard core, tell-it-like-it-is, no sugar coating. This stance is supremely direct but not mean.
- **Professor:** Cool, high advocacy, factual, "this is how it is," "when you do X, you get Y."
- **Best Buddy:** Highly empathetic: "I've been there, I know how hard it is."
- **Guru:** The wise knowledgeable one, often used by consultants, has a touch of Professor but is less linear and more about overview, has a touch of warmth and heart. This stance is the expert with a heart and high enrollment.

I find that combining stances is super helpful. For example, if a team member has performed well in the past yet has repeatedly struggled for a prolonged period of time, the following approach could work:

> Leader: "Pierre, you are a huge asset to this organization; your performance has been exceptional in the past. I know how great you are [Mommy]. But we've had this conversation twice already and nothing has changed. *We need you back on track now.* Don't make me put you on probation [Drill Sergeant]. Hey, I've been where you are. . . . I know how hard it is when you're having the personal life changes that you are [Best Buddy]. Please help me to help you bring back the awesome guy I know you are [Mommy]."

> Leader: "Susan, I'm curious as to why we aren't getting the results we had wanted in our recent marketing campaign. What do you think got in the way of our results? What could we have improved? [Anthropologist]."

Based on Susan's response, you could either use Professor with a prescriptive solution—if she is in her Critter State—or, if she's in her Smart State, Guru could be used to work together on a solution.

Best Buddy and Professor are another good combo, especially when you want to empathize with someone yet state the facts as they are. The key is that two stances build connection and safety (Mommy and Best Buddy), two stances spur action (Drill Sergeant and Professor), and two stances help people solve their own problem (Anthropologist and Guru). Ask yourself the following:

Which stances do you default to?

Which do you find uncomfortable?

Good. Now let's step into the discomfort zone.

How do the different stances feel? The goal is to see how different stances are necessary for us to be powerful in our lives—whereas most of the time people take on only one or two stances that are triggered by outside circumstances. Learning how to mix and match behavioral stances will increase your range and flexibility in your business, and the person with the greatest range and flexibility in any system will influence it the most.

We'll talk more about behavior flexibility in part 3, in chapter 9.

Stuck Spot: the Flailing Sales Manager

The chief revenue officer of a Fortune 500 company called us because Sam, their VP of sales, was repeatedly missing his quota. The company's food services division was intent on reaching the $500 million revenue inflection point that year and Sam's performance was critical.

Once we dug in, we learned that Sam had been a salesperson himself in the past. Of the six stances leaders use, the stance he consistently defaulted to with his team was Best Buddy. When a salesperson missed her number he would empathize with her, share her pain, and ultimately send the message that missing one's number "this time" was okay. This led to repeated misses because the Best Buddy stance validates the behavior of the recipient. It is not the stance to use when driving quota-based salespeople to performance!

Diagnosis: Low influence due to inflexible and inappropriate stance.

We worked with Sam and helped him adopt a combo of Mommy and Drill Sergeant when working with his sales team. Now Sam gives quota-missers a message like this: "X, you're a great salesperson. I've seen you knock it out of the park in the past [Mommy]. But now it's time to bring your A game. Like *now*. We need immediate action on your performance or I'm going to have to let you go / put you on probation [Drill Sergeant]. Help me help you, X, to return to your terrific performance. I know it's inside you. . . . I've seen how awesome you are [Mommy]."

Sam's team soon began to step up, and with his new style flexibility Sam was also able to effectively use the Accountability Equation, Needle Movers, weekly tracking, and a new incentive plan with consequences for missed quotas (see chapter 5 on accountability for more details) to ramp up his team. The results are already in: Sam's division reached the $500 million inflection point and they're now creating a new strategy—outlining their people, money, and model changes—to reach $1 billion within six years.

Make sense? Now it's your turn! Let me know how your experiment with stances goes.

How to Get Influence Fast

In closing, I want to mention one final tool: influencing phrases. These are especially helpful when a person is in their Critter State and we want to help them feel safe enough to shift out of it.

There are three influencing phrases:

1. **"What if"**: When you use this preface to an idea/suggestion, you remove ego and reduce emotion. You're curious—not forcing a position, but kind of scratching your head and pondering. This enables someone to brainstorm more easily with you.
2. **"I need your help"**: We call this a dom-sub swap, because when the dominant person uses it, they are enrolling the subordinate person and asking them to rise up and swap roles. This is an especially effective phrase when you want a person to change their behavior or take on more responsibility.
3. **"Would it be helpful if"**: When someone is stuck in their Critter State and spinning or unable to move forward, offering up a solution will help them see a possible course of action or positive outcome.

Now that we understand the basics of influence and some key techniques, we'll dig in to advanced influence tools in the next chapter.

▼

Twitter Takeaways

Find these helpful? Tweet them to your tribe and reference #SmartTribes as the source. Thanks!

- You can learn to step onto the Map of another to influence outcomes and/or increase trust and connection by using rapport-building techniques.
- The Outcome Frame is an exceptional tool for helping ourselves and others to edit our Maps.

- The more influential you become, the more you are putting yourself at the service of your team. Real influence is about empowering others.
- 90% of our reactions are emotional, and our emotions respond four hundred times faster than our intellect.
- Our unique "map" of the world houses our beliefs, shapes our identity, determines our behavior, both the things we want to do and our responses to what happens to us.
- Most of us are highly predictable. We react in predictable ways, we have predictable patterns of behavior, we have predictable speech. How predictable are you?
- Use Influencing Phrases to shift people into their Smart State: What if, I need your help, Would it be helpful if . . .

Assess

- Whom do you naturally have rapport with? What is the result?
- Whom would you like to have more rapport with? What could it mean to you—what would a possible result of increased rapport be?
- What rapport tools do you already naturally use?
- Which would you like to add to increase your influence?

Act

- Review the section on stances above. For the next week, experiment with the three stances that are most uncomfortable for you. How did your results differ? How did your ability to influence change? What scenarios did you use them in?
- In addition to working with the three stances most unfamiliar to you, start using two or more of the rapport tools each day.
- Incorporate one or more of the influencing phrases into your leadership tool kit.

• • •

ROI

Note how the rapport tools affect your performance and influence with others. Thanks to these and the additional tools in the next chapter, our clients have reported:

- Sales are closed 22–50% faster.
- Sales close rate is increased by 44% or more.
- Marketing messages are 37–301% more effective.
- New products and services are created 29–48% faster.

Resources

Helpful resources in this chapter include:

- The first four rapport-building techniques
- The six stances
- The three influencing phrases

Go to www.ChristineComaford.com/resources and download the kits that will be most helpful for you. We think the following kits would be a good start:

- Assess Your Team's Performance
- Marketing Optimization and Focus
- Streamlining Your Sales Funnel

Also check out the following in the appendix:

- Presence Process
- Seeking Balance via Connection

7.

META PROGRAMS
Make Loaded Dice Even Heavier

Meta Programs are one of the most potent rapport techniques, because they enable us to most deeply step into someone else's world. They allow us to access a part of the subconscious mind that is often unavailable in general social transactions. Rodger Bailey did groundbreaking work on Meta Programs in the workplace.[1] Shelle Rose Charvet's excellent book on Meta Programs, *Words That Change Minds*, is a deep source based on Rodger Bailey's work, if you want to invest a chunk of time.[2]

What we love about Meta Programs (it's our favorite influencing—rapport—technique!) are the somewhat staggering results one can get in short order—weeks or months. When we train sales teams on Meta Programs in selling scenarios, they close sales up to 50% faster. When we work with marketing teams, their messages resonate with prospects more deeply and faster—up to 301% more effective. Also, demand generation increases by up to 237%. Why? The same reason for all the results: we build greater trust with the recipient of the message by profoundly increasing safety, belonging, and mattering. Meta Programs are so sophisticated that some people find further instruction beyond the scope of this book will be required for mastery. That said, if you practice these techniques they will improve your communication and influence profoundly. They're fascinating and fun too.

Let's dive in.

SmartTribe Accelerator #4.5:
Meta Programs for Advanced Influence

Meta Programs are the filters through which we see the world, the ways our brains process the world and determine how we react to it. When we speak to someone using their Meta Programs, they not only hear what we're saying but they also feel they belong with us, that we are similar, that we "speak the same language." We're safe. We're of the same tribe. We want the same things. Sounds like good rapport, right?

Meta Programs are equally useful whether the person you're addressing is a team member, a board member, a sales prospect, a client, or the recipient of a marketing message. Speaking to someone using their Meta Programs enables us to step onto the Map of their world, ensures profound rapport, and leads to outcomes that are better for everyone—while fostering deep connection and trust.

Meta Programs are a spectrum: we don't usually fall all the way to one side or the other as an absolute. We'll usually have a lot of one and less of the other and fall somewhere between the two poles. Meta Programs are contextual, meaning that you may have one filter set in the context of work, another set when it comes to money, and yet another for romantic love, and so on, though we generally have an overall set for how we approach life.

Being able to understand and use Meta Programs in a variety of business scenarios is a strong and relatively undetectable way to influence others and outcomes. You'll need more detail to master this, so please see the Resources section at the end of this chapter.

There are sixty Meta Programs, according to Rodger Bailey's research, yet I have noticed that six are key to affecting outcomes:

- **Toward-Away.** Are you motivated to go toward a goal or away from pain? Think salesperson versus accountant: what criteria do they "sort" with?
- **Options-Procedures**. Do you like to have many options and choices or prefer a proven step-by-step process? What feels right to you?
- **General-Specific.** Do you feel comfortable with a high-level overview or do you want specific details? When describing something, do you start with the details or the summary?

- **Active-Reflective.** Do you have short sentence structure and high action, or do you want to think about things first, using longer sentence structure with many clauses?
- **Internal-External.** How do you know you've done a good job? Through external feedback or internal monitoring?
- **Sameness-Difference.** Do you prefer to stay with one company in one position for a long time or do you need a change in your working environment or role every six months to two years? There are also options between these two poles.

Let's break this down into more detail.

Toward-Away

	Toward	Away
Description/motivations	Motivated to achieve goals; to move forward; get what they want.	Motivated to solve problems and avoid risk taking / pain.
Advantages	Have lots of energy and momentum; inspire others to action; provide a compelling vision for others to latch on to.	Are the "voice of reason, not;" grounded, and realistic. They appreciate and understand the risks and what problems may occur.
Disadvantages	Toward people can be so goal-oriented that they don't focus on / appreciate / accept what is needed to make goals happen—all the work others will have to do that takes time. Toward people are often impatient; they will already be focused on the next goal so may not appreciate the achievement of the current goal.	Away people can be too cautious and may appear resistant to take action.
Influential words	"Get," "attain," "achieve," and synonyms of these.	"Avoid," "prevent," "assess," "consider," and synonyms of these.
Often found in	CEO, sales, business development, software development, design.	Accounting, operations, risk management, nonlitigation legal roles.
Possible conflicts	The Toward person may discount the Away person's point of view, may think he's dragging his feet or just doesn't "get it." The Away person may feel the Toward person is all about the vision, when what really matters is the execution of it and risks. Disrespect on both sides can cause tremendous tension.	

Here's the approximate distribution of this Meta Program in the American workforce:

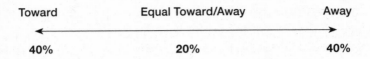

Decoder Question: To find out whether a person is Toward or Away, ask, "What do you want in your work [or something else important to them]?" Keep asking questions like "What else do you want?" or "What else is important?" Notice what descriptor words they use, and tabulate. Be sure to keep a written running score so that your own Meta Programs don't filter what you hear—if you have an extreme bias, you may hear one mention of the other pole as extreme when actually the person is middle-of-the-road.

Options-Procedures

	Options	Procedures
Description	Motivated by choice, possibility, variety; will give you a list of criteria they want.	Motivated by following a proven and reliable process; will lay out a step-by-step process or need one provided for them.
Advantages	See many ways to solve problems, to implement ideas, to make things happen. The world is their oyster.	Very reliable and consistent in delivering results by following specific procedures. You can count on them to not cut corners and to follow the rules.
Disadvantages	Options people can create so many choices that they get stuck and don't act, or they present so many options to their team that their strategy and priorities become unclear—again slowing results.	Procedures people can often suffer from rigid thinking and tunnel vision. They stress when a clear procedure isn't provided or when procedures across the company are inconsistent or differ for similar tasks.
Influential words	"Variety," "choice," "possibility," and synonyms of these.	"The right way," "series of steps," "reliable process," and synonyms of these.

Often found in	All roles, though they often gravitate toward anything with "design," "development," or similar words in the title that indicate there is room to operate differently. Options people love to create processes for *other* people to follow.	All roles, though they often gravitate to accounting, manufacturing, legal, engineering, and other process-driven fields.
Possible conflicts	When an Options person presents too many choices, a Procedures person may shut down or feel so overwhelmed that he won't know how to proceed. When a Procedures person tries to force a process on an Options person, conflict will arise. A better approach is to "interview" the Options person in order to determine the procedures he needs.	

Here's the approximate distribution of this Meta Program in the American workforce:

Options	Equal Options/Procedures	Procedures
←		→
40%	20%	40%

Decoder Question: To find out whether a person is Options or Procedures, ask, "Why did you choose your current work/job/car?" An Options person will respond with his criteria, or a list of features or traits—for example, for a car: "It gets great gas mileage, it's black, and it has fast acceleration." A Procedures person will respond with a story that details a process through which the car was the end point: "Well, you know, it's a funny thing. My old car was breaking down all the time and my aunt Sue was visiting and . . ."

• • •

General-Specific

	General	Specific
Description/motivations	Motivated to summarize and think at a high level. Looking at the forest.	Motivated by details and sequences. Knows how many trees the forest contains, how many leaves each tree has, and the variation of their bark.
Advantages	Have broad perspective and can see the net-net, don't get caught up in the details, keep momentum moving.	Catch the crucial details that if overlooked could be problematic. Provide thorough execution and can answer questions with the key components to ensure decision making is accurate.
Disadvantages	A person can stay at too high a level and fail to execute, or fail to help others execute and be perceived as glib or vague. They may also make decisions while lacking crucial data.	Getting lost in the details and losing sight of the goal, the overall strategy, the priorities, the results.
Influential words	"Overview," "the big picture," "in general," "the point is," and synonyms of these. Start with setting frame or context.	"Specifically," "exactly," "precisely," and synonyms of these. Start at detail level and build to conclusion.
Often found in	CEO and all leadership roles, market/strategy development roles.	Engineering, legal, accounting, operations, market research roles.
Possible conflicts	A General person may gloss over details or not take the time to drill down on them, either dismissing the Specific person for being too nitpicky or for bringing up info that seems (to the General person) irrelevant. The Specific person may see the General person as not committed, unrealistic, or irresponsible.	

Here's the approximate distribution of this Meta Program in the American workforce:

General	Equal General/Specific	Specific
◄——————————————————————————————————————►		
60%	25%	15%

Decoding: There is no specific question to find out whether a person is General or Specific. However, you can ask questions like "How do you brainstorm challenges at work?"; "How do you solve problems?"; "Describe your weekend"; "What do you do for fun?" Notice which influential words they use, and if they start with specific details or with an overall summary statement.

Active-Reflective

	Active	Reflective
Description/motivations	Motivated to take action immediately, charge ahead.	Motivated to analyze, wait, and react when appropriate.
Advantages	Can be counted on to take the initiative, rally the troops, go-go-go. Value getting it done yesterday, no matter the cost.	Carefully assess input before taking action. Value getting it right over getting it done.
Disadvantages	An Active person can be too hasty in her forward momentum, not considering the risks involved. She also can be so itchy to act that she leaves out key people or acts out of the optimal order of tasks or projects.	A Reflective person can get perfectionistic, get stuck in analysis paralysis, or be too slow to take action. These people can be seen as less valuable, as not having leadership potential—which is untrue.
Influential words	"Get it done," "now," "don't wait," and synonyms of these.	"Consider," "could," "understand," "think about," and synonyms of these.
Often found in	Sales and other customer facing/initiating roles.	Research, analysis, customer service, service.
Possible conflicts	There is high potential for the Active person to dismiss the Reflective person as a passive order taker. This is far from the truth. The Reflective person can see the Active person as acting for the sake of action and not thinking her actions through.	

Here's the approximate distribution of this Meta Program in the American workforce:

Active	Equal Active/Reflective	Reflective
←		→
15–20%	60–65%	15–20%

Decoding: There is no specific question to find out whether a person is Active or Reflective. Ask questions such as "How do you solve problems at work?"; "How do you discover opportunities or challenges?"; "When do you know when your attention is needed?"; "How do you learn new things?" Listen for sentence structure as well as their use of influential words.

Internal-External

	Internal	External
Description/ motivations	Motivated to decide on own internal standards—don't expect them to seek or respond to external praise and incentives.	Motivated by external praise and rewards.
Advantages	Are generally very self-directed and "low maintenance."	It's easy to incentivize them with bonuses, prizes, recognition. It's very clear where they stand.
Disadvantages	An Internal person can be tough to manage and incentivize, and there will be problems if his internal bar of excellence / accomplishment is out of sync with his manager's.	An External person can be too dependent on outside praise or attention and may be perceived as draining and needy, or as working only for the prize and not for the mission. He can be too easily swayed by the last external input or the input from the highest-ranking person, even if it's wrong.
Influential words	"What do you think," "it's up to you," and synonyms of these. This is where special challenges or cool projects can be effective versus public recognition and rewards (which he doesn't care about—he already knows he's great at his job).	"Others will notice," "feedback you'll get," "raise your profile," "award," "acknowledge," and synonyms of these.
Often found in	Engineering, manufacturing, legal, and leadership roles.	Sales, marketing, and other outward-facing roles.
Possible conflicts	An Internal person may disregard or even mock company incentives and cultural rituals of recognition if he feels the culture is too concerned with them (and key accountability structures aren't in place). An External person can become too dependent on prizes/praise and may lose motivation without constant incentives.	

Here's the approximate distribution of this Meta Program in the American workforce:

Internal	Equal Internal-External	External
40%	20%	40%

Decoder Question: To find out whether a person is Internal or External, ask, "How do you know you've done a good job?" An Internal person will know because of something—often a feeling—inside herself. Answers will often be something like "I just know." An External person will refer to other people's opinions/quotes/testimonials, facts and figures, recent promotions, or other forms of public recognition.

Sameness-Difference

	Sameness	Difference
Description/ motivations	Motivated by what's in common, and by preventing change.	Motivated by radical, total, revolutionary change.
Advantages	Maintaining the status quo can be helpful if the changes haven't been well thought out or don't have a clear and compelling communication strategy. You can count on them; you know where you stand and what they'll be doing for a long time.	Innovation and evolution are key in several fields. The person driving this state of dissatisfaction with the status quo can be a key leader and can bring tremendous energy.
Disadvantages	A Sameness person can be excessively fearful and rigidly resistant to change—which is often simply growth.	A Difference person can be so pro-change that things are broken simply to provide the buzz of changing them, usually at unnecessary expense and time spent. Sometimes it's hard to know what they stand for.
Influential words	"Consistent," "same," "stable," and synonyms of these.	"Disruptive," "change," "different," "revolution," and synonyms of these.
Often found in	Roles with high stability and routine.	Leading-edge research and development roles across technology and other fields.
Possible conflicts	These two roles can clash when management is in one Meta Program and staff is in the other. This is a fairly rare scenario, however. See below for the most common Meta Program regarding change.	

About the Sameness/Difference Motivation Trait: This Meta Program has a wide range, from Sameness through Difference with identifiable sorts in between. It is essentially about how people tolerate change.

Sameness people like change about every twenty-five years. Difference people will prompt change every six months to two years. Change does not mean they leave, but they do have to recommit.

In the middle of these two ranges is Sameness with Exception, which is where most American workers fall (change every five to seven years: the famous "seven-year itch"). This Meta Program has some change tolerance as long as it makes sense—for example, they are fine with cherry Coke because it's good old Coca-Cola, just with cherry added. Likewise, Coca-Cola Zero is good old Coke with the calories removed. If consistency is provided and extra good things are added or annoying things are removed, the Sameness with Exception person will thrive. This is why we coach leaders on using the words *growth, progress,* and *evolution* as opposed to *change.* Change can hurl us into our critter brain, whereas growth messaging puts us in our prefrontal cortex, where we want to solve puzzles, have visions, and be creative.

The most unusual iteration is Sameness with Exception and Difference. This person wants some consistency with the occasional revolution—a rare combo. They average liking change every three to five years, with five to seven years in some contexts and up to two years in others.

Here's the approximate distribution of this Meta Program in the America workforce:

Same	Same w/Exception	Same w/Exception+Difference	Difference
5%	65%	10%	20%

Decoder Question: To find out where a person is on the range of Sameness to Difference, ask (and the wording on this one is very important), "What is the relationship between your work this year and last year?" Most people will look at you blankly and ask you to explain the question, but don't, just ask them to answer as best as they can and repeat the question verbatim. A Sameness person will look for all the things that are the same even if they moved from accounting to sales, changed companies, and physically moved to a different state. "Well, I'm still working with numbers and doing calculations. I still wear the same clothes . . ." A Difference sort will tell you everything is completely different even if the only change was to move to the next cubicle: "Oh, my God, it's a completely different worldview!"

Stuck Spot: the Too-Talkative CFO

Sarah, a CFO at a Fortune 1000 insurance company, talked too much. She thought she was being thorough and showing that she was on top of matters. The CEO, however, thought Sarah was insecure, energy draining, and time consuming, and he did his best to avoid her. By the time Sarah reached out to us, it was clear her days were numbered.

We could see instantly that Sarah was communicating from her Meta Programs and not from the CEO's and subsequently losing more rapport and credibility with every interaction.

Diagnosis: Meta Program mismatch and hijack.

To help Sarah we first had to uncover why the CEO's attitude triggered Sarah's need to talk excessively, a hijack just like we described in chapter 2. Using the Outcome Frame (see chapter 6 on influence) we found that this was a general pattern Sarah employed in times of stress, a pattern that evolved in kindergarten, where she learned the hard way to speak up or be perceived as a failure. Once we saw how Sarah's behavior was delivering the opposite result, we helped her create new behaviors that would be more effective.

Objective: Increase the CFO's Ability to Communicate Her Talent and Ideas to the CEO.

We first taught Sarah how to step into the CEO's world by determining his Meta Programs. This would enable her to speak in a way that the CEO could actually hear.

Meta Programs of CEO: Toward, Options, Active, Internal, General, and Sameness with Exception

Sarah, on the other hand, was wired up to filter through the Meta Programs of Away, Procedures, Reflective, External, Specific-General, and Sameness. You can see that they were almost a complete mismatch! No wonder Sarah couldn't get through. This dramatically affected *how* Sarah needed to communicate.

Influencing Language Example: Sarah now crafts her finance-oriented messages to the CEO using the CEO's Meta Programs, which builds rapport and means that the CEO actually hears the messages. Sarah also watches the CEO's reaction to her words, and if the CEO starts to shut down, Sarah quickly summarizes (Active/General). Further, since Sarah now knows that the CEO processes information visually, she brings simple visual tools like charts and graphs to their meetings.

Here is an example of how Sarah changed her language to build rapport with the CEO's Meta Programs of Toward, Options, Active, Internal, General, and Sameness with Exception:

> Original Sarah: "I've been looking at our teleconference bill and I think we could save 30% or more. We need to analyze conference services and cloud possibilities because I'm concerned we're overspending by at least $15,000 per month and I'm thinking through the best process to identify a qualified but more cost-effective service [Specific/Away/Reflective]."

> Posttraining Sarah: "I want to speak with you about our goal to not just double revenue this year but also increase profitability. I have some cost-cutting measures I'd like to propose. Are you interested [Toward/General/Proactive (note short sentence structure) / Internal]?"

Outcome: Sarah's rapport and trust with the CEO has skyrocketed, and the CEO recently told us he thinks Sarah is one of the best hires he's ever made.

More Examples of Meta Program Use

Here are a few client scenarios in which understanding the recipients' Meta Programs and speaking in them yielded terrific results.

Objective: VP of Operations Wants the Regional Manager to Lead More Proactively.

The VP of operations of a Fortune 500 restaurant chain wants several of her regional managers (RMs) to take on more responsibility. Most of them are too set in their ways, but she's identified one rising star who's young and formative. The VP sees amazing potential and wants to develop the RM's leadership skills and make her the poster child for employee growth. The problem is that she's a little timid and seems to be starving for praise. The VP has been trying to help the RM along for months but can't seem to reach her, and she's about ready to give up.

Meta Programs of Regional Manager: Toward, Options, General, Reflective, External, Sameness with Exception

Influencing Language Example: The VP needed to change the way she spoke with the RM. "I need your help [enrolling]—I think we have a great opportunity [Toward, Options] for raising your profile [External] and developing you as a leader [Toward]. I'd love your help [becoming submissive and letting RM become "bigger" to emotionally enroll her and get her to feel more powerful] in increasing our collective commitment [Toward] to weekly one-on-ones with staff [Specific] so we can catch problems before they occur [Reflective], and discover new ideas and options [Options] to reduce ticket times and increase guest experience numbers [General]. We're doing well and I know we can do better [Sameness with Exception]. I'd love your help [enrolling again] in achieving our numbers [Toward] and we'd both enjoy the recognition [External] that would come from it. This is a fantastic opportunity for our region to shine and set the standard to inspire others [External]."

Outcome: The regional manager stepped up and is now leading one of the top two regions in the country.

Objective: Help Bob Rise Up as a Leader, and Become More Entrepreneurial and Less Risk-Averse.

Five partners started a mid-sized East Coast manufacturing business. Today, one of them is leading the company, one is just about to retire, and two others are pulling their weight. The fifth, Bob, is slacking. He's getting paid like a partner but he's not bringing in as much revenue as the others.

Bob's Meta Programs: Toward, Procedures, Specific, Reflective, Internal, Sameness with Exception

Influencing Language Example: "I need your help [enroll and engage]. What could we achieve if we fostered a deeper sense of leadership and built a more entrepreneurial culture [Toward]? Would you like to help me with this [Internal]? We could develop some specific plans and procedures [Procedures, Specific] to take our culture to the next level [Toward]. To do this we partners need to go to the next level too. How could we do this [Internal]? Will you watch the team [Reflective] at the leadership training this month and let me know what you think we could add to motivate them and turn up their intensity level [Sameness with Exception]?"

Outcome: Bob is reinvigorated as a partner. He's taking on a greater leadership role in the firm and is far more accountable.

Objective: Stop Clare's Excessive Checking in with Her Boss About Every Tiny Detail.

Clare is extremely competent. She really wants to please her boss at a mid-sized West Coast professional services firm but is quite insecure—she can't seem to do anything on her own. She's constantly dropping in on the CEO to make sure what she's doing is okay and to get the boss's approval. The CEO became so frustrated that he thought about firing Clare but doesn't want to because Clare is incredibly good at her job.

Clare's Meta Programs: Away, Procedures, Specific, Active, External, Sameness with Exception

Influencing Language Example: The CEO received coaching to take advantage of Clare's competence and give her increased responsibility and projects. At the same time, Clare's feeling of autonomy and confidence needed boosting so that she wouldn't need so much outside praise. "I need your help [enroll and engage]. I trust you [External] and know you have the answers. It would be a great help to me if you could create whatever processes and procedures [Active, Procedures, Specific] you need to feel confident completing your assignments without my involvement [Away]. You're doing great and I know you can rise to the next level this year [External, Sameness with Exception]. Can you help me understand the info you need to do your work without feeling you need to check in with me [Active, Specific, Procedures, Away]?"

Outcome: Clare's boss has gained fifteen hours a week—time he used to have to spend stroking Clare or giving her orders. Clare has been promoted.

Objective: Create More Effective Marketing and Sales Messages.

A Global 2000 accounting company had been marketing new out-sourced back-office services to their finance and operations clients for three years. Results had been dismal, with only five sales in the past eighteen months.

Meta Programs of Prospects: Away, Procedures, Specific, Reflective, Internal, Sameness with Exception

Influencing Language Example: We worked with the client to shift their marketing from Toward (exciting and focused to an entrepreneurial mindset—like the client's team was) to Away (more cautious and focused on stability and safety). Marketing messages now incorporate the following:

- Away: Solve problems the right way with a stable, solid approach, such as we're finance people just like you and we are all about assessing the situation carefully, then forming an action plan based on our forty years of experience. We're in this together as an extension of your back office.
- Procedures: We follow reliable procedures to prevent errors and optimize efficiencies. We understand the value of consistent high quality results, and our proven seven-step process ensures you get the most for your investment.
- Specific: Each month we'll provide you with a detailed report of the work we've done together to ensure all critical success factors are being monitored. Here's a sample format. Want more or different information? No problem. Let's meet and design the reporting to support your business best. We all know how essential accurate financial data is to executive visibility.
- Reflective: We're finance professionals, and so we don't make hasty decisions. We'll follow our four-step assessment process to analyze your exact needs and to create a plan to support your key objectives.
- Internal: You know your value—and so do we. You'll make the right decision as to whom your strategic back-office partner should be. We know it's a long-term relationship, and you'll drive the decision-making process, just like all of our other clients do.

- Sameness with Exception: Working together will simply take the low-value minutiae off your plate, so you can focus on the strategic and high-impact, high-leverage work you specialize in. We're here to take your headaches away.

Outcome: The company has expanded from basic outsourced accounting to payroll and a plethora of additional financial services, warehouse management, and logistics services. In the past the company would generate approximately one hundred unqualified leads per month. In the first six months, after launching and ramp-up of similar campaigns with Meta Program messaging, they generated 210 *qualified* leads per month, sales closed 48% faster, and their sales close rate has increased by 55%.

Objective: Close Sales Faster—and Make Them Stick.

An Inc. 5000 technology company has a challenge—they sell to three different sets of Meta Programs. There are the enthusiastic executives, the operations folks who'll have to live with the solution, and the technology team that will have to integrate the software solution into their corporate infrastructure. Often the operations and/or technology staff would kill or stall the deal when the company thought it was "all good."

Meta Programs of Executive Prospect: Toward, Options, General, Active, External, Sameness with Exception

Meta Programs of Operations Prospect: Away, Procedures, Specific, Reflective, External, Sameness with Exception

Meta Programs of Technology Prospect: Away, Procedures, Specific, Reflective, Internal, Sameness with Exception

Solution: First we did both loss and close cycle analysis to find out what percentage of sales the company lost and why, as well as how long sales took to close. We quickly saw that we needed to change up the team that was calling on each account. Here are the highlights of the multifaceted and highly successful solution:

- Identify our sales and executive team by the sales roles they could play: energizer (for rapport with the Toward and Active client-side executives), stable (for rapport with the operations folks), and tech (for rapport with the technologists). Several of the company team could play multiple roles.

- Increase attention to meeting agenda and client-side team mix. Bring both an energizer and a stable always, as operations usually pop in unannounced. Add a tech when needed in person or via phone or Skype.
- Rewrite marketing messages and request for proposal cover letters with Meta Programs.
- Develop a visual process so the prospect could see the eight stages a company goes through in implementing the company's solution. This made the operations and technical folks feel increased safety, belonging, and mattering.
- Assign a client concierge to each account immediately after close. This role would make sure the right answers and expertise would get to the client promptly, as well as manage the client's experience of the technology company (yes, using Meta Programs!).

Outcome: The Inc. 5000 tech company now enjoys sales that stick—when they are closed, they are indeed closed and have a 97% retention rate. They are closing sales 27% faster, and their customer satisfaction rate is up by 31%.

This is just a preview of how using meta programs keeps everyone in their Smart State and builds your ability to influence tremendously. It's a lot to think about, so I encourage you to find an executive coach versed in this rapport technique to help you achieve mastery.

▼

Twitter Takeaways

Find these helpful? Tweet them to your tribe and reference #SmartTribes as the source. Thanks!

- Meta Programs help us access parts of the brain generally suppressed in cultured daily life.
- Meta Programs are a terrific tool for influencing outcomes while fostering safety and belonging.
- Use the words *growth*, *progress*, and *evolution* as opposed to *change*. Change can hurl us into our critter brain, whereas

growth messaging puts us in our prefrontal cortex, where we want to solve puzzles, have visions, and be creative.

- How can you connect more deeply with someone today?
- Where would you like to increase your influence? On others and outcomes? Home, work, or both?
- Use the Outcome Frame: What would you like? What would having that do for you? How would you know when you had it?
- Who are the stakeholders in your career? How have you stepped into their world to support them today?

Assess

- What are your Meta Programs? Pick two contexts—for instance, in business overall, your romantic relationship, parenting, leading others, or your finances. How do your Meta Programs vary in these contexts?
- Think of three stakeholders in your work and life—perhaps a key client or prospect, your boss or a key board member, your right-hand person. What are their Meta Programs? Use the table above to figure them out.
- Now look at your marketing material, key website copy, or even your standard request for proposal cover letter. Are you speaking in the Meta Programs of your prospect?

Act

- What outcome would you like to create with the stakeholders you identified above? Craft a communication from the examples in this chapter and test it. How did it go?
- Rank by priority the areas where you'd like to increase your influence. Start communicating in the Meta Programs of the recipients of your messages. What is the result? Do you experience more collaboration, easier outcomes, and greater connection?

ROI

Meta Programs take a while to learn and are absolutely worth it. Our team uses them with one another, with our clients and partners, and in our personal lives. Here are some benefits our clients have experienced, thanks to communicating in Meta Programs and using other influencing techniques:

- Marketing demand generation increases by 31–237%.
- Sales are closed 22–50% faster.
- Sales close rate is increased by 44% or more.
- Marketing messages are 37–301% more effective.
- 100% increase their ability to significantly influence others and outcomes.
- 100% report the ability to apply communication techniques and thinking styles both at home and at work and a resulting increase in personal fulfillment.

Resources

Helpful resources in this chapter include:

- The six types of Meta Programs

Go to www.ChristineComaford.com/resources and download the kits that will be most helpful for you. We think the following kits would be a good start:

- Special Report: The Five Critical Mistakes That Halt CEOs
- Streamlining Your Sales Funnel
- Marketing Optimization and Focus
- Assess Your Team's Performance

8.

SUSTAINABLE RESULTS
How to Have More Energy Than a Teenager

Have you ever made a big change, only to see your results disintegrate before the change is locked in? How many people lose weight only to regain it, reorganize their company but divide instead of unite the team, or reach a huge milestone yet drive everyone to burnout? Sustainable results require several components to succeed and "stick"—for starters, we need to get in and stay in our Smart State.

Think of the seemingly boundless energy of a teenager. Why are they this way? Is it because they often see endless opportunity and possibility? Yes. In my experience with shifting the energy level of executives, the more we focus on the outcomes we want to create, the more we get in our Smart State. The more we trigger the reward center of our brain (primarily the ventral striatum), the more we move forward with eager anticipation of great things to come. The more we use our tools for focus, clarity, accountability, and influence, the more structure we lend both to ourselves and our teams to get in and stay in our Smart State. And once there, we slide into the Jet Stream of our compelling and emotionally engaging vision, which continues to pull us forward.

It's a self-fulfilling prophecy. How cool is that?

Energy management must be intentional, conscious, and a key priority. The world is full of brilliant minds unable to fulfill their mission because they burned out first. Moving through an inflection point requires intention, energy, and heart. Manage your energy and you'll continue to surge forward. Don't and beware the backward slide.

SmartTribe Accelerator #5: Sustainable Results

Sustainability is about creating win-win agreements with ourselves and others.

Being sustainable is essential to lead; to feel balanced, centered, and not burned out; and to help your team feel that you are their protector—and they are thus safe and can be loyal. So why is being sustainable sometimes hard? Because being truly sustainable means we can no longer self-sacrifice or expect our team members to. Sustainability prevents burnout.

Let's have a look at how sustainable you are.

Take out a piece of paper and divide it into three columns. Label the first column "Gain Energy," the second "Lose Energy," and the third "Mixed." This is your Energy Allocation Chart (see table 8-1).

TABLE 8-1. ENERGY ALLOCATION CHART

Gain Energy	Lose Energy	Mixed (% totals 100)
Exercising	Filing/paperwork	Paying bills (80/20)
Achieving goals	Working with negative people	Georgianne (30/70)
Working with positive people	Driving in traffic	
Hanging out with friends		
Learning new skills		

In the first column, fill in people, activities, and things that add energy to your life. So if your daily exercise program helps you stay clear, that would go in the Gain Energy column. Maybe overall your children, your dog, and your best friend go into that column.

Now move to the second column. What things drain you? List those here under Lose Energy. For me it's administrative tasks: filing,

scheduling, minutiae. There are also certain people who drain you—
the ones who make you want to take a nap after interacting with them.

Last, let's fill in the third column. These are the people, activities,
and things that are mixed in your energy allocation—sometimes they
help you gain energy, and sometimes they drain you and you lose energy. What percentage is each? Maybe a colleague is mostly in the
Gain column, but when he interrupts you while you're trying to focus
he goes into the Lose column. Is he fifty-fifty in the Mixed column?
What percentage would you assign? Can you identify the context or
specific part of the interaction that's draining?

Once you have your list, it's time to be focused and present to
what's really happening. What is your energy allocation? How many
Gain items did you have versus Lose and Mixed? How are you contributing to the energy loss you are experiencing? Are you giving unclear expectations (practicing clarity and explicit communication)?
Are you creating unrealistic or non-agreed-upon deadlines (utilizing
the Accountability Equation)? Are you paying attention to both your
Map and theirs?

Now let's create an action plan. Can you get rid of anything in your
Lose column? Can you delegate any activities that drain you? If it's a
person, does he have to be in your life? You may have to put fences
around people who are pulling you away from your goals; in the case
of relatives, you may have to strategize (with your significant other or
siblings) about how to reduce the points of stress. For example, one
client had to negotiate with his spouse to manage his in-laws differently at the annual family function they hosted so that everyone
shared the load and he didn't feel like a servant.

The stuff in the Mixed category is the most tricky. Your strategy
will probably be more about moving the items from the Mixed list
firmly into the Gain list. In my example above, I have someone else
pay my bills and Georgianne is no longer in my life.

Conducting this energy management audit is something we encourage SmartTribes to do regularly. It's a great way to engage all the
SmartTribe Accelerators in one practice.

• • •

Stuck Spot: the Command-and-Control CEO

Dan, a CEO at a mid-sized northeastern financial services company, always seemed to be on edge. Whenever one of his key executives came to him for advice, he would impatiently bark out an answer. When Dan came to us, he complained that he had a culture of order takers, not leaders, and he wanted us to change this.

When Dan created an Energy Allocation Chart, almost all his direct reports (and there were a lot of them) were in the Lose category, a few were Mixed with low gain percentages, and none was in the Gain category. Further investigation revealed that Dan was losing energy through his own perceived necessity to tell everyone exactly what to do and when to do it—and he was disappointed when they either did it differently (their own way) or not at all.

Diagnosis: Unsustainable energy allocation due to need to control, additional problems with focus (not listening or being present), and Accountability Equation (no owner agreement and no consequences).

Using the Outcome Frame from chapter 6, we uncovered that Dan grew up in a family of very impatient people, so that trait was pretty well imprinted on his Map. In the company, the ability to follow orders efficiently was prized.

We had to start by helping Dan to be more patient so that he could affect the core culture of the company to value problem solving. But before we could add patience to his Map, we had to make sure that doing so wouldn't cause a disconnect with his family (remember ecology from chapter 6?).

By constantly commanding, or advocating, Dan was unwittingly creating order takers. We began editing patience into his Map by teaching him that anytime someone came to him for advice, instead of telling him or her what to do, he should ask questions—at least five for each order he wanted to give. He had to show his team that he wanted them to solve the problem and take the initiative.

This was excruciating at first, because he had to rein in his impatience and enroll his executives in finding solutions, in considering what the risks and benefits might be, what resources they would need, and so on. But as Dan began asking these questions, he learned that his people were smarter and more creative than he had thought—he simply hadn't given them an opportunity to use these skills before. By rewiring himself and practicing new behaviors (inquiry instead of advocacy, making clear requests, asking for promises, and agreeing to consequences), he was able to shift the overall culture of his organization.

Within four months, Dan's executive team was taking more initiative, accepting greater accountability, and—since they were empowered to truly own their work—they were stopping by his office a lot less often. It had also become increasingly obvious that he had too many direct reports, and from his use of inquiry, he knew exactly how to reorganize and how to create the right message so that his team stayed motivated. This freed up eight hours per week for Dan.

Increasing foundational SmartTribe Accelerators meant sustainable results. Dan's executives are now nearly all in the Gain column of his Energy Allocation Chart (or at least in the Mixed category) and are working together as a real team—a SmartTribe.

Where Sustainability Gets Squashed

All leaders want to spend more time on strategic work than on drudgery. Where, oh where, does all our time go? As we discussed in chapter 3, you need to take a moment to consider high-value activities (strategic activities, things you are really good at, places where putting your energy pays off huge dividends) versus low-value activities (work you don't do well or that someone else would be better suited for, tasks that are draining or should be ditched/delegated/deferred). What percentage of your week is allocated to each? Does the percentage change when averaged over a month?

Another huge energy drainer that slurps away sustainability is triggered emotional reaction from our Critter State, instead of a chosen response from our Smart State. The critter brain will send us into fight/flight/freeze until we know how to manage it. A fascinating exercise is to note how often you react in ways that are automatic and unconscious versus responding in ways that are based on full conscious choice.

What Role Do You Play?

We all have a default role, one we learned early in life. This role has shaped our lives, and it is often what prevents us from fostering sustainability in ourselves and in our teams. Our role may keep us (or others) in our Critter State, or cause unhealthy dependency.

You might think of your default role as the lens you look through, a lens that colors everything you see. These three default roles were first created by Dr. Stephen B. Karpman, and his article detailing these roles won the Eric Berne Memorial Scientific Award in 1972.[1] David Emerald then expanded the work,[2] and I've taken it a step further.

There are three basic default roles that people lean toward:

- Victim
- Rescuer
- Persecutor

These three roles are interdependent (there must be a Persecutor for there to be a Victim for the Rescuer to save), and together they make up what we refer to as the Tension Triangle (figure 8-1).

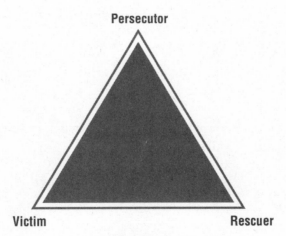

Figure 8-1. The Tension Triangle

When we're in the Tension Triangle, we're problem-focused and tend to see things as shown in figure 8-2.

Being problem-focused sucks our energy, leads us to look for ways to allocate blame, and feels constricting, like a jacket that's too tight. When we're problem-focused, we are in our Critter State, in fight/flight/freeze. Stay there too long and you'll slide into apathy. And that takes a *lot* more energy to shift out of!

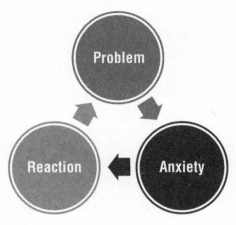

Figure 8-2. The Problem-Focused Lens

Another drawback to being problem-focused is that it can interfere with the way we see Maps—ours and others'—and it can lead to self-sabotage, which we generally do (unconsciously) in two ways:

- We get stuck in our Map and miss the opportunity to add new helpful resources to it to help ourselves grow.
- We stay in our Map while trying to influence another—but if we don't step into their Map, we will likely miss powerfully influencing outcomes.

With the tools I'll provide below, we can switch to being outcome-focused, which looks like figure 8-3.

Figure 8-3. The Outcome-Focused Lens

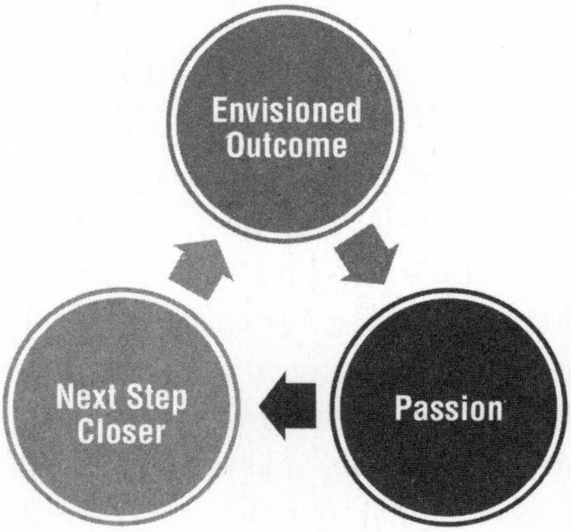

Being outcome-focused feels very different. It's empowering and energizing, and fills us with confidence. It firmly places you in your Smart State, where possibility, choice, innovation, love, and higher consciousness are abundant.

Not sure whether you're problem- or outcome-focused? Think about the questions you ask:

Problem-oriented questions	Outcome-oriented questions
What's wrong?	What do we want?
Why is this happening?	How will we create it?

As we mentioned in chapter 6, UCLA found recently that 50–70% of an organization's collective emotional state is determined by its leaders. This means that if we're problem-focused, our people likely are too. It's essential to learn the tools to shift your organization and yourself from problem-focused thinking to outcome-focused. This means shifting from the Tension Triangle to the Empowerment Triangle, from the left to the right, in figure 8-4.

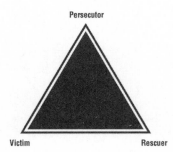 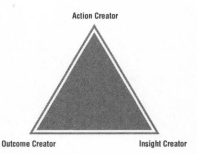

Figure 8-4. Shifting from Problem-Focused to Outcome-Focused

As we shift from a problem- to an outcome-oriented focus and culture, something super cool happens: we shift ourselves.

The charts below outline the basic process for moving from the Tension Triangle to the Empowerment Triangle. By understanding your primary tension orientation and flipping it to its positive empowerment counterpart, you will encourage your team members to be internally motivated, to be fully accountable for their area, and to take ownership of the organization's key initiatives.

The positive counterpart of the Victim is the Outcome Creator. All Victims want a certain outcome—this is what they are complaining about. Our goal is to help them focus on what they want, as opposed to what they don't have or don't like. The positive counterpart of the Rescuer is the Insight Creator. All Rescuers want to help save the Victim, yet they have tremendous skills that can help them enable the victim to save themselves. The positive counterpart of the Persecutor is the Action Creator. The persecutor wants to get momentum, to get a result. Once they learn to create the action they seek in a healthy way, the drama can end.

How to Shift Your (and Another's) Role from Tension to Empowerment

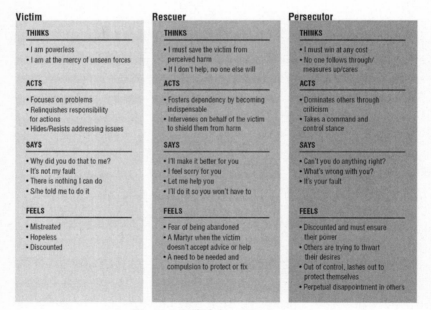

Figure 8-5. Shift from Tension . . .

Here's how to do it:

1. Identify each role you and the other person are playing.
2. Speak to the other person as the positive counterpart. For

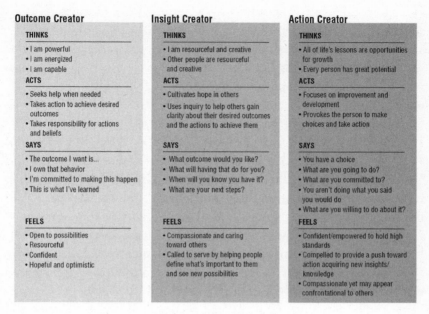

Outcome Creator	Insight Creator	Action Creator
THINKS	**THINKS**	**THINKS**
• I am powerful • I am energized • I am capable	• I am resourceful and creative • Other people are resourceful and creative	• All of life's lessons are opportunities for growth • Every person has great potential
ACTS	**ACTS**	**ACTS**
• Seeks help when needed • Takes action to achieve desired outcomes • Takes responsibility for actions and beliefs	• Cultivates hope in others • Uses inquiry to help others gain clarity about their desired outcomes and the actions to achieve them	• Focuses on improvement and development • Provokes the person to make choices and take action
SAYS	**SAYS**	**SAYS**
• The outcome I want is... • I own that behavior • I'm committed to making this happen • This is what I've learned	• What outcome would you like? • What will having that do for you? • When will you know you have it? • What are your next steps?	• You have a choice • What are you going to do? • What are you committed to? • You aren't doing what you said you would do • What are you willing to do about it?
FEELS	**FEELS**	**FEELS**
• Open to possibilities • Resourceful • Confident • Hopeful and optimistic	• Compassionate and caring toward others • Called to serve by helping people define what's important to them and see new possibilities	• Confident/empowered to hold high standards • Compelled to provide a push toward action acquiring new insights/ knowledge • Compassionate yet may appear confrontational to others

Figure 8-6 . . . to Empowerment

instance, if he is in Victim mode and you tend to be a Rescuer, ask the questions of an Insight Creator (the positive counterpart of the Rescuer). If he is in Rescuer mode and you tend toward Persecutor, speak to him as an Action Creator. If he is in Persecutor mode, ask him what actions he wants—speaking like an Insight Creator often works best.

3. Hang figures 8-5 and 8-6 in your office. Enroll others in helping you shift to your positive counterpart. This promotes candor and increases connection among colleagues.

It works. We see cultures shift from seeing the problems to actively creating the outcomes they desire in record time. Even the most confirmed Victims shift to Outcome Creators.

Stuck Spot: The Talented Rescuer

Suzanne was a human resources manager at a large East Coast consumer packaged-goods company. And she was always exhausted and close to totally burning out. Why was she always exhausted? Let's find out.

We had Suzanne start a tally. Within the first week, nine Victims came to Suzanne for rescue. Their complaints were varied: colleagues withholding information; there was someone they didn't like; the cafeteria needed more healthy food; and so forth. None was an issue Suzanne needed to be involved in.

Diagnosis: Suzanne was a Rescuer.

When taught how to shift from Victim/Rescuer/Persecutor to Outcome Creator / Insight Creator / Action Creator, Suzanne quickly realized why she had always felt so exhausted: she rescued people all day long. She needed to get to work tracking her rescuing patterns.

Suzanne learned how to stop trying to solve other people's problems and instead give people efficient techniques to help them solve them on their own. She enlarged our Shift from Tension to Empowerment charts and hung them on her office wall. Whenever Victims came to her, she told them she had realized she was a Rescuer and enrolled them to help her shift this. In mere weeks, a number of former victims were focused on the outcomes they wanted, and signs like the one in figure 8-7 started popping up on cubes all over the company.

Figure 8-7. Progress at Suzanne's Company

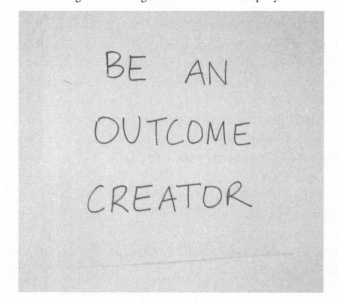

Suzanne is no longer in the rescuing business. In fact, she was promoted to director of human resources. She recently presented her strategic vision for human resources to the C-suite and received significant accolades. We're betting she'll be a vice president within two years.

Sustainability is about having enough energy to enjoy what you're doing, getting consistent high-value results, and creating win-win agreements with people. When our team sees that we can work hard and not have to sacrifice ourselves to the cause, their sense of safety, belonging, and mattering skyrockets. We *can* have fun and fulfilling lives and careers (yes, both!). The tools in this chapter help you ensure it.

------------------------▼------------------------

Twitter Takeaways

Find these helpful? Tweet them to your tribe and reference #SmartTribes as the source. Thanks!

- Sustainability is about energy management, or about finding out what drains us or puts us in conflict, and clearing it.
- We all default to one prevalent role, that of Victim, Rescuer, or Persecutor (or a combination). These roles can easily be flipped to Outcome Creator, Insight Creator, or Action Creator to increase results and performance, reduce stress, and improve relationships.
- The more we focus on the outcomes we want to create, the more we get in our Smart State.
- The more we trigger the reward center of our brain (primarily the ventral striatum), the more we move forward with eager anticipation of great things to come.
- The more we use our tools for focus, clarity, accountability, and influence, the more structure we lend both to ourselves and our teams to get in and stay in our Smart State.
- Energy management must be intentional, conscious, and a key priority. The world is full of brilliant minds unable to fulfill their mission because they burned out first.

- Make 3 columns. Label the first column "Gain Energy," the second "Lose Energy," and the third "Mixed." Now fill them in. This is your Energy Allocation Chart.
- Being problem-focused sucks our energy, leads us to look for ways to allocate blame, and feels constricting, like a jacket that's too tight.
- Being outcome-focused is empowering and energizing, and fills us with confidence. It firmly places you in your Smart State, where possibility, choice, innovation, love, and higher consciousness are abundant.

Assess

What role do you often default to? (Hint: What role or roles did you play in your family as you were growing up?) What is the result of being in this role—what does it "cost" you?

- What role do you think the key stakeholders in your organization see you in? How do you reinforce this?
- What percentage of your energy is spent on high-value activities?
- What did you learn from your Energy Allocation Chart?

Act

Here's an exercise that will help streamline where your time is spent:

- Write down your top three business priorities.
- Check your calendar to see if each appointment / time allocation is supporting your top three priorities. For each appointment / time allocation, score 1 for yes; 2 for sometimes yes / sometimes no, mixed, or uncertain; 3 for no.
- How many 2s and 3s do you have? You may need to get more clarity or change the scope of the 2s to get them out of the ambiguous category (or reduce it at least). Now work on getting rid of the 3s (ditch, delegate, or defer) and ensuring 70%

or more of your time is spent on 1s. Plan out a process for getting 70% of your time allocated to high-value activities. How quickly can you make this shift?

This exercise will help you find more time for Smart State strategic work that is exciting and energizing, versus low-value and draining.

- Enlarge and hang the Shift from Tension to Empowerment charts on your wall. Whenever someone comes to you in a problem-focused state, tell them the problem-focused state you want to shift yourself from, and enroll their help.

ROI

The return on investment in managing your energy as a precious resource is profound. By fully shifting from problem focus to outcome focus, here's what you could gain:

- Individuals become 35–50% more productive.
- Individuals are 67–100% more emotionally engaged, loyal, accountable, and ownership-focused.
- 97% tangibly contribute to increasing key executive strategic/high-value time by five to fifteen hours per week.

Resources

Helpful resources in this chapter include:

- Energy Allocation Chart
- Tension to Empowerment Process
- Mapping top three business priorities to time allocation (see Act section above)

Go to www.ChristineComaford.com/resources and download the kits that will be most helpful for you. We think the following kits would be a good start:

- Managing Your Energy to Keep Your Momentum
- Knowing What You Want and How to Get There: Why Are You Building This Company?
- Increasing Accountability and Ensuring Goals Are Met
- Assess Your Team's Performance

Also check out the following in the appendix:

- Values Exercise
- Silence Practice Techniques
- Energy Recall

PART THREE

BUILDING
YOUR OWN
SMARTTRIBE

AN ACTION PLAN

9.

HOW CHANGE HAPPENS
The Three Essential Keys to Starting Your SmartTribe

B y now we've learned how we can get in and stay in our Smart State, and how the five SmartTribe Accelerators help make this happen. We've also learned how useful the Smart State is and how high the ROI is to our business. Next we're going to tie everything together. In this chapter, we'll cover how change happens, so you'll understand the process you're about to undergo to build your SmartTribe. It's time to reap the rewards of all your work.

There are three core concepts you need to know about change as your organization starts applying the SmartTribe Accelerators. Understanding the *logical levels of change*, clarifying your *present and desired states*, and identifying the stage of the *organizational change process* you're in will smooth out your experience of creating your Smart-Tribe. And all of these core change concepts have to do with addressing the system, not the symptoms.

Focus on the System, Not the Symptoms

When a problem presents itself, most executives look for point solutions, such as "What problem/situation do I need to change?" This is tactical thinking. Maybe you want your people to be more accountable, your salespeople to sell more, your engineers to innovate better, or your client-care team to service accounts better.

Solving these problems is addressing the symptoms, not the system. It is not looking at the situation *systemically*. Consider the difference between Western and Eastern medicine: Western is problem- and point-solution-oriented, and Eastern is preventive- and systemic-solution-oriented.

The key to making lasting systemic change is having a clear understanding of where you are now—understanding your stuck spots—and clarifying where you want to be—your smart spot.

Key #1: The Logical Levels of Change

The process of getting from Stuck to Smart involves working at six distinct levels of change. These levels were first identified by the social scientist Gregory Bateson.[1] I see them as concentric rings (see figure 9-1). In the environment, behavior, and capability rings, we have the symptoms. In the beliefs, identity, and core/culture rings, we have the system.

You can start at the outside, making changes to environmental factors, and those changes may work their way inward and ultimately affect the core/culture. But sometimes those changes can be superficial because they are dealing with symptoms and not the system. What happens when you work only at the symptom level? You'll have to deal with the next symptom, and the next symptom, *forever*—because it's the system that causes all the symptoms.

To get out of this endless cycle, we need to look at how our business is being impacted on multiple levels. Then we can operate with far more impact once we treat the system—not just the next symptom.

Outside in is a valid approach if creating a fresh new environment will facilitate the deeper, more profound changes to come. Even redecorating the office or moving people around can often shake things up so people become conditioned to or ready for greater change. Yet we have found that if you start inward at the core/culture and align the outer layers with the inward changes, your changes will be deeper and lasting. The inside out approach takes a bit longer initially. Here, we start with our mission, vision, and values first, followed by our cultural identity and beliefs. Then we move outward to the easier changes.

Whether you work outside in or inside out—or, better yet, both simultaneously to get the quick "hits" while the deeper work percolates—you absolutely have to make sure the environmental changes support the cultural changes, and vice versa.

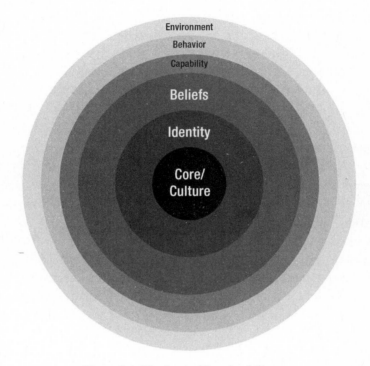

Figure 9-1. The Logical Levels of Change

The rings move from the environmental symptoms, or those that are the easiest to implement but often have the least leverage, on the outside to the systemic core/culture norms, or the hardest to implement but most profound, at the center. Let's go through all six levels in detail.

Environment. This is your physical and energetic environment. Think back to the home you lived in as a young child: this is where your environmental expectations were set. In your workplace there is a physical environment and an emotional one. Is the vibe in your office positive, collaborative, "got your back," team-oriented—keeping your team in their Smart State? Or is it negative, fearful, "everyone for themselves," silo-oriented—triggering Critter State? Making environmental changes—especially physical ones—can be permanent or temporary: you can move to a new office or location, temporarily change rooms, or just take a walk.

When you were a child, did you ever move to a new house? Did that have much of an effect on your relationship with your parents? Probably not. And getting up right now and changing seats—which is an environmental change—wouldn't change your relationship with your parents either. Your relationship with your parents is part of the culture of your family (at the very center of the bull's-eye), which is why reorganizations (which are also a type of environment change) rarely improve an organization's culture. A new job title and new responsibilities may help your career and move you to a new office, but they don't fundamentally change who you are. To affect the whole system, an environmental change has to be aligned with the core/culture at the center.

It is well known that Steve Jobs spent a lot of time on and was very particular about the design of the Pixar building. In order to maximize interactions among team members, he created an atrium that everyone would have to walk through several times a day. He even opposed some of his executives' requests and located all restrooms in that atrium. By aligning his environment with his expected outcome (more team member interactions that eventually led to a dynamic team cohesiveness), Jobs profoundly affected Pixar's innovative culture. The environmental change was totally in line with the company's core/culture.

Now imagine if you put the most cost-driven, conservative, bureaucratic company you can think of—one with a culture of "don't waste time chatting with people"—into that same building. Would they become innovative? I doubt it. The environmental change would have to be aligned with a cultural change to be effective.

Behavior. Suppose you make a New Year's resolution to go to the gym. How long does that last? (Three weeks for about 90% of people, per Dr. Howard Rankin.)[2] You want to lose five pounds, so you stop eating dessert for a few days. That's a behavior change. A few days later, that tiramisu or cheesecake looks really good . . . and there you go.

Behavior change can work, but often it is woefully transitory. If it is not supported by an identity change of "it's a lot more fun to skip dessert and have vibrant energy," the change doesn't trickle in and other concerns will preempt the change. We need to have a deep desire to make changes that stick, otherwise we'll default to patterns that have kept us safe (and are familiar), but not necessarily happy.

One of the best examples of successful behavioral change can be seen in the agile software development process. The behavior protocols reflect a fundamental value change, expressed in the written directive "people before process." For example, in agile software development, the entire team is involved in estimation—as opposed to a top-down approach where one or two managers make the decisions based on very little and often incomplete information. When learning the agile development estimation process, team members may feel self-conscious about not knowing enough, and it takes time for the team to gel and feel comfortable having healthy conflict. The result is that team members learn to value one another's input more. Through this behavioral/process change there is a culture shift away from achievement and toward team experience and collaboration, and for the individuals involved, there is also an increase in self-value.

Capability. Behaviors done in a particular context to create a particular outcome are a capability. This is about acquiring new skill sets. For example, public speaking is a capability that involves the behaviors of standing, walking, and speaking. But the capability of public speaking involves a lot more than just those behaviors. When you put them together in context and add the desired effect of appropriate communication or motivation, you have the true substance of the capability: presenting oneself appropriately and with authority; connecting deeply with the audience and monitoring their interest, energy, and absorption levels; speaking clearly and with passion; and using your body and voice to illustrate and accentuate.

Most people spend their time and energy trying to change the outer three rings: environment, behavior, and capability. They focus on the symptoms of a problematic culture, not the system. The system cannot change the organization unless the inner rings are also engaged.

Beliefs. These are decisions about how the world works and your place in it. In an organization, this translates into rules—rights and wrongs, shoulds and shouldn'ts, goods and bads, cans and can'ts—what is acceptable, or culturally normal. Beliefs are more deeply rooted in our subconscious, so you'll need to do quite a bit of digging (aided by the skillful use of the neuroscience techniques we'll be getting to soon) to unearth them and then change them.

Want to quickly identify a few of your organization's beliefs? Notice your results, notice the behaviors that led to those results, step into an observer position (as if someone else did what you did), and ask yourself, "What would someone *have to* believe to have that experience?"

Examples of beliefs could be "It's easy to propose new ideas here," "Management cares about the team here," or "The company policies are fair."

Identity. This is simply a collection of beliefs about *ourselves*. Or, in the case of an organization, its identity is what its stakeholders (team members, customers, suppliers, and investors) say about it.

If you haven't seen Michael Apted's *Up* documentary series, check it out.[3] In 1964 a group of filmmakers interviewed fourteen seven-year-olds. They reinterviewed the same people when they were fourteen, twenty-one, twenty-eight, thirty-five, forty-two, and forty-nine. It's amazing that more than forty years after we first met the children, they're essentially the same. Their identities were established almost at birth—and so are most people's. But if you learn to edit your Map, you'll be able to give yourself more choice and possibility in life.

So what's your identity? Fill in the blank to learn what your beliefs about yourself are: "I am _____." Powerful? Confident? Loved? Influential? Smart?

A company identity comprises its brand image as well as what team members believe about the company. When team members describe their place of work, what do they say? *"My company* is _____." Innovative? Team-oriented? Old-fashioned? A family business? Young? Full of possibility?

What's your company's identity? Fill in the blank to learn what your team's collective beliefs about the company are: "We are _____." Market leaders? Perpetual learners? All about client delight?

Core/Culture. We've finally reached the juiciest part of all, which is, in a sense, a microcosm of the whole Map, the world as it is right now. *Core* applies to individuals—it's who you are, what you stand for, what will last if everything else is stripped away. *Culture* refers to organizations—it's what the company believes about its executives, its rituals, the behaviors that are rewarded or punished, the function and dysfunction.

Again, change can happen inside out or outside in, but if you change one aspect and it is not aligned with the other, it is rarely effective.

Key #2: Understanding Your Present State and Desired State

"This place is killing me," Jeff the CEO said to me. "I need more than 35% growth this year and my executives are expert finger pointers."

He'd joined a mid-sized health-care company one year ago and had been breaking up executive brawls ever since.

Here's a typical example: The VP of marketing wanted to spend more money on campaigns. The CFO objected—he hadn't seen ROI on the current campaigns. The CFO came to Jeff, the CEO, complaining that the VP of marketing was "impossible."

Then what happened?

Jeff would mentor the CFO on how to better communicate with the VP of marketing: how to inquire and understand the expenses better, maybe even how to hold him accountable for his expenditures. And then . . .

Tactics would be developed.

Tactics would be deployed.

Fleeting temporary change would occur.

Because tactics are stupid.

When it comes to human behavior, tactics don't truly, deeply change anything. The next time there's an executive clash, they'll be right back in Jeff's office. *Tactics treat the symptom instead of the system.*

To change the system for either an individual or a company, we must first understand the present state (where we currently are) and the desired state (where we want to be).

Let's get back to Jeff and his brawling CFO and VP of marketing. Here's the present state as Jeff described it:

Core/Culture: A culture where low accountability, execution, and distrust reign.

Identity: Jeff feels like a Rescuer. The VP of marketing feels powerless and not valued—a Victim. The CFO feels frustrated and blocked from getting what he needs—also a Victim. And the two of them see each other as Persecutors.

Beliefs: CEO: "This won't/can't change." The CFO distrusts the VP of marketing and thinks he's a flake. The VP of marketing feels that "it's me versus them."

Capability (limitation): No accountability or execution structures; no communication rhythms.

Behavior: Resist accountability; inconsistent execution; blame one another.

Environment: Silos of information; cliques; executives who avoid one another physically.

Remember how we said that systems are the reflection of a company's leaders? Well, this is a classic example. The present state existed because the company's core/culture supported it. Jeff was working only at the environment, behavior, and capability levels and missing the belief, identity, and core/culture levels. In other words, he was treating the symptoms instead of the system. So the executive fights continued, as they had for five increasingly unbearable years.

When we were brought in, the first thing we helped Jeff see was how he was helping to perpetuate the present state.

Here's what Jeff's desired state looked like:

Core/Culture: Culture makes communication safe, and encourages and rewards accountability. Trust and a sense of belonging are essential.

Identity: CEO: "I am a problem resolver, and an Insight Creator. I help team members work out challenges with one another. The CFO and VP of marketing feel valued and understood."

Beliefs: CEO: "My team members are competent and caring." CFO and VP of marketing: "This is where I belong"; "We are a team."

Capability: Accountability and execution structures; rewards and consequences; SOPs to improve efficiency and reduce conflicts.

Behavior: High accountability, execution, and trust. Team members find solutions together.

Environment: Meetings, teams, and physical space are structured to maximize collaboration.

You'll see that in both the present and desired states, the core/culture is essentially a summary of the rest of the layers. So even though it looks like a CFO/VP of marketing challenge, it quickly becomes obvious that we're really looking at a company-wide cultural (systemic) challenge. Change the core/culture, and everything in the surrounding rings changes right along with it.

Had the company had a collaborative, trusting, high-communication culture, the tension between the CFO and VP of marketing and other executives would likely not have existed—or it would have been resolved without the CEO's involvement.

Here's how Jeff replaced the present state with the desired state. First, he led the executive team through our Logical Levels of Change diagram and had the team collectively design their desired state using the process in the Assess section at the end of this chapter. Next, he "chunked down" the most important systemic changes with our help. Here's what we did:

Found out what truly motivated the team. We interviewed a diverse sample of the company's population across the organization chart (all levels, all areas of the company, all tenures) to find out what the team was truly motivated by, what their complaints were, what they wanted to keep, and what they wanted to let go of in the culture. From there we had a realistic view outside the executive suite and knew what was and wasn't working.

Reduced victim thinking and increased rapport, accountability, and execution. With this knowledge we taught them the accountability and communication structures (chapter 5), helped them shift from Victims/Rescuers/Persecutors (chapter 8), and helped them increase rapport alignment and influencing outcomes (chapters 6 and 7). Now the team had a new set of capabilities to add to the environment and behavior changes they were undergoing.

Set consistent communication rhythms. When the company's executive team set up consistent meeting and communication rhythms, execution and connection began to improve. Company-wide Needle Movers with rewards and consequences sweetened the results. Rituals to bring the company together and contests to encourage an environment of celebration as business objectives were met were the icing on the cake. This step helped edit beliefs and expand identity.

Reinforced the culture change. Coaching the CEO and executive team in how to create and reinforce the change they wanted at the core/culture level worked wonders. We used the same Map-enhancing techniques we discussed in chapter 6 to help each executive change their most challenging behaviors, see into their blind spots, and enhance their vision.

Fourteen months later this company had been transformed to its desired state. Oh—and their growth wasn't 35%, as the CEO wanted. It was 42%.

When you work solely at the environment, behavior, and capability levels, you are working on the symptoms. When you work on identity and belief, you are working on the system. This is true leadership.

Remember: changes at all inner levels result in changes at all the outer levels.

You gain two things from the present state/desired state model:

1. You know where to go to work, because you know what is most crucial to shift.
2. You clearly understand how you are creating the culture.

Key #3: the Organizational Change Adoption Path— What to Expect When You're Expecting People to Change

Not everyone in your organization is going to embrace and celebrate change. Every leader knows that the biggest challenge with change is resistance. But what most miss is that resistance is simply the first stop on the quest for the holy grail: a new standard.

From my work with hundreds of successful entrepreneurs, top executives, and political leaders, I've learned that organizational change is a continuum. It's predictable, it can be guided, and here is how it works.

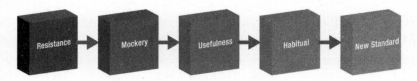

Figure 9-2. Organizational Change Adoption Path

First, people start with resistance. Why? Because thanks to Rodger Bailey's terrific research on Meta Programs, we know that 65% of Americans can tolerate change only if it is couched in a specific context. If we're looking at our Meta Programs from chapter 7, the context is "Sameness with Exception." This means the "change" is really just an improvement to what we are already doing: the bad stuff is being removed, and good stuff is being added. Seriously—this is the best way to package a change message. And don't use the *c* word—say "growth" (or a synonym) instead.

Many clients ask us if this path is linear. The answer is both no and yes. As you change the overall culture, different departments and different people will be working on different things. They may be in different places, and sometimes people regress, especially if they get hit with one change after another. However, you can usually walk around the company, speak with your tribal leaders (those key thought leaders or de facto leaders in your organization), and get a good sense of where you are overall.

Company Z, a food services firm with nearly $400 million in annual revenue, was changing their business model. It was a big change—they were dumping one entire business unit and launching a new one. The team was none too happy about it. Some were fearful because they were employed in the now defunct business unit, and they'd have to learn new skills. The change was essential, though, because due to market conditions the former unit would never become consistently profitable. The CEO, Jessica, did a masterful job managing the organizational change.

First, she had the entire company trained on how change works and how to expect their brains and emotions to react. Jessica's assistant had the CCA Organizational Change Adoption Path (figure 9-2) expanded, printed, and posted in the conference room so everyone could openly acknowledge where they were in the process. When people get a chance to visualize the change and how they fit into it and when they feel they are being included—think safety, belonging, and mattering—they can get on board faster.

Next, she laid out a plan to help the team navigate the five phases.

- **Resistance:** This phase can pass fairly quickly when the leader stresses the "same with exception" nature of the change. That's exactly what Jessica did.
- **Mockery:** I love this phase! It means people now have some emotional investment. They are past disinterest and resistance and we can engage them in telling us what they object to. We acknowledged their concerns and asked for their help in fixing what in the CEO's growth plan was so "lame." We asked for their agreement to follow the plan once their fixes were made. This led to . . .
- **Usefulness:** The mockers worked through the revised plan with Jessica and us and some even—gasp!—acknowledged what parts of it were useful. A few mockers insisted on a few more edits, and the CEO agreed to about half of them with,

again, the agreement of their support. This is the most important step, because when something is truly useful, the vast
majority of people will use it again, leading to . . .

- **Habitual:** Now we've got the team members using something
  repeatedly, almost without thinking. Which leads us to . . .
- **New Standard:** The behavior is becoming integrated into
  how they behave and setting a new behavioral standard.

This process can take months to years, based on how the leader
manages the Organizational Change Adoption Path. With our client
above, the change took seven months to filter through all the remote
offices—this is speedy.

How the Brain Handles Change: The Pain and Reward Networks

But what if the above doesn't work? Most of us have seen unsuccessful
change scenarios—when change failed because too many key stakeholders got stuck in a perpetual resistance-mockery loop. Why? Generally the case is that not enough rapport skills are being used by the
change initiator—the degree of safety, belonging, and mattering has
not been amped up and divisiveness reigns. If this happens to you,
revisit rapport in chapters 6 and 7, enroll the key stakeholders from
the start, and use your influencing phrases from chapter 8.

It's essential to consider that we don't really fear change per se; instead we resist the pain that we perceive will come from change and
we fear the unknown. This is why leaders need to be aware of both the
social pain and social pleasure (or reward) networks. I'll simplify the
fantastic work of Naomi Eisenberger at UCLA and George Kohlri-
eser of IMD with this short summary.

Eisenberger has found that our social attachment system piggy-
backs onto our pain system, likely to promote survival. If we look at
the most effective method of punishment for centuries—exile—where
we have lost all safety, belonging, and mattering, this makes sense.
Also consider how dependent we humans are on others for years after
birth. If separation from a caregiver/leader is a threat to survival, feeling "hurt" by separation may be an adaptive way to prevent it. When

team members feel their leader doesn't care about them they experience social rejection, which lights up the pain network. Further, when a team member perceives unfairness, the pain network lights up. Yet another reason for a high communication, high accountability, high transparency culture.

If our pain network is lit up, we are in our Critter State—our survival is at stake. As we know, emotional pain can last years longer than physical pain, so until the culture is healed, the separation and pain continues.

When an organization or individual feels their leader deeply cares for them, they trust their leader to help them navigate change. Both the leader's and team member's reward networks light up as a result of giving support and receiving support, respectively. We actually see reduced perception of threat in the brain, even when the change/risk is profound because we know we're not alone. As leaders, we can also light up the reward center by treating others fairly, collaborating, and cultivating team members via Individual Development Plans. Activating our reward center helps us stay in our Smart State.

That said, I want to stress that the brain isn't so mechanical. Pain is a complex experience that involves many aspects of the brain. There is the physical pathway of pain (and reward), which then sets off reactions in the emotional and cognitive parts of the brain that significantly influence our experience. We get the pain signal but then we start to interpret it and emotionally react to it, which then alters the experience. My aim is for leaders to raise their awareness around how they can influence others more effectively by reducing activity in the pain network and increasing activity in the reward network.

Twitter Takeaways

Find these helpful? Tweet them to your tribe and reference #SmartTribes as the source. Thanks!

- As leaders, we are constantly looking at what we are doing. It's time to start looking at who you are *being*. What is it you are not yet doing *and* are not yet being?

- Change happens on a continuum. Resistance is not a bad thing—it's the first step to a new standard. Remember the Organizational Change Adoption Path!

- Leaders have the ability to light up the pain or reward networks of their teams. Support and fairness are the best ways to help team members experience social rewards and stay in their Smart State.

- Is the vibe in your office positive, collaborative, "got your back," team-oriented—keeping your team in their Smart State? Or is it negative, fearful, "everyone for themselves," silo-oriented—triggering Critter State?

- Behavior change is often transitory. If it is not supported by an identity change it doesn't trickle in and other concerns will preempt the change.

- Want to quickly identify a few of your organization's beliefs? Notice your results, the behaviors that led to those results, step into an observer position (as if someone else did what you did), and ask yourself, "What would someone *have to* believe to have that experience?"

- What's your identity? Fill in the blank to learn what your beliefs about yourself are: "I am _____." Powerful? Confident? Loved? Influential? Smart?

- What's your company's identity? Fill in the blank to learn what your team's collective beliefs about the company are: "We are _____." Market leaders? Perpetual learners? All about client delight?

- When you work solely at the environment, behavior, and capability levels, you are working on the symptoms. When you work on identity and belief, you are working on the system. This is true leadership.

Assess

Now let's work on your company's present and desired states.

———

Create the following template on a sheet of paper or an online document:

Level	Present State	Desired State
Core/Culture		
Identity		
Beliefs		
Capability		
Behavior		
Environment		

We'll do this together, one level at a time. We'll get more bang for our buck by using a neuroscience technique involving eye movement.

- Close your eyes and look up and to the left. You're walking through your company: see, hear, and feel yourself in the halls. What is the environment like—emotionally, physically, energetically? As soon as you've got it, open your eyes and write it down in the "Present State" column for environment.
- Repeat this process, always looking up and to the left as you engage as many senses as possible and step through the levels of behavior, capability, beliefs, identity, and core/culture, one at a time. If your firm has multiple locations, chances are good each one has slightly different present and desired states. You could do this exercise with the executive of the given site to get a more accurate read.
- Take a break and stand up. Shake your arms out, roll your shoulders, move.
- Now let's create your desired state. Close your eyes and look up and to the right this time. You're walking through your company in the desired state: see/hear/feel yourself in the halls. What is the environment like—emotionally, physically, energetically? As soon as you've got it, open your eyes and write it down in the "Desired State" column for environment.
- Repeat this process, always looking up and to the right as you engage as many senses as possible—see, hear, feel yourself in the desired state—and step through the levels of behavior, capability, beliefs, identity, and core/culture.

- Look at your present state—really look at it. This is what you created. It's a mirror of who you are. The system is now functioning without you—it's on autopilot. Now look at the two columns for present and desired states. How different are they? How much change do you need to cause?

Act

- Whom do you need to be to create your desired state? How will you become that? Work with your executive coach to effect the above changes.
- What are the current identities and key beliefs of the greatest stakeholders on your team? What are three ways you can help them shift their identities and beliefs to be more positive and powerful?
- Where are you on the Organizational Change Adoption Path? Where is your team? Apply the techniques you learned in this chapter to help them move one to two steps further to the right, or, if they're at a new standard, to help them move their colleagues further.

ROI

When we understand the dynamics of the Logical Levels of Change, present and desired states, and the Organizational Change Adoption Path, we can help move our team forward much faster. Here is the ROI we've seen companies experience from managing change with these three tools:

- Individuals become 35–50% more productive.
- Revenues and profits increase by up to 210% annually.
- Individuals are 67–100% more emotionally engaged, loyal, accountable, and ownership-focused.
- 97% tangibly contribute to increasing key executive strategic/ high-value time by five to fifteen hours per week.

- 63% receive a promotion to a role with increased responsibility and management of others within six months of applying our techniques via coaching and training.

Resources

Helpful resources in this chapter include:

- The Logical Levels of Change
- Present states and desired states
- The Organizational Change Adoption Path

Go to www.ChristineComaford.com/resources and download the kits that will be most helpful for you. We think the following kits would be a good start:

- What Do You Stand For? Defining Personal Values
- Leading from the Inside Out
- Knowing What You Want and How to Get There: Why Are You Building This Company?

Also check out the following in the Appendix:

- Presence Process
- Silence Practice Techniques
- Values Exercise
- Seeking Balance via Connection

10.

MAKING YOUR SMARTTRIBE A REALITY
The Four Factors of a Sustainable SmartTribe

By now it's clear that a SmartTribe is truly compelling for your business—and we know change (even if we call it "growth") can be difficult. Now that you understand the three theoretical keys to change, let's get more practical. What can you do to optimize both organizational effectiveness and the adoption of the SmartTribe Accelerators in your company?

The Four Factors of a Sustainable SmartTribe

In your own life, you need to balance a variety of factors in order to live a fulfilling, authentic, and sustainable life. These factors might include physical health, family relationships, career, spirituality, time to yourself, and others. (By the way, if you'd like to enhance your ability to lead a balanced life, see the section in the appendix titled Seeking Balance via Connection.) If one of these key factors is out of balance, your whole life becomes out of balance and unsustainable.

The same is true for your SmartTribe. It's not enough just to understand and practice the SmartTribe Accelerators. I've found that a sustainable SmartTribe is found at the intersection of four key components:

- Behavior
- Leadership Effectiveness (via embodying the SmartTribe Accelerators)
- Organizational Effectiveness
- Mission, Vision, and Values

The point at which all intersect is the point at which we have the highest level of effectiveness overall.

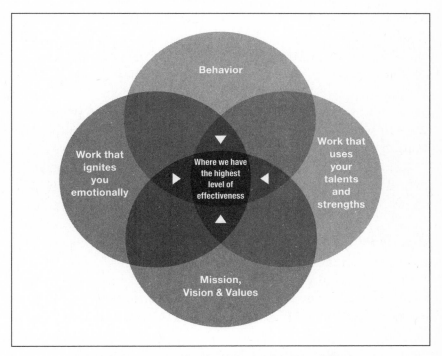

Figure 10-1. Four Factors of Sustainable SmartTribes

We've spent most of the book covering three of the four elements, so I'll summarize quickly. Our *behavior* depends primarily on our sense of safety, belonging, and mattering, and, as we discussed in parts 1 and 2, is affected by whether we're in our Critter State or our Smart State and governed by our beliefs, identity, resources, and all the other goodies on our Map of the world. But it's important to note the nature of behavior. More and more we're realizing that behavior is quite predictable. For example, per Dr. Howard Rankin's work,[1] two of the aspects that govern behavior are having a personally compelling "why" behind the desired behavior plus understanding how habits are made and broken (see figure 9-2, the Organizational Change Adoption Path in chapter 9). Can one always align his or her behavior with the mission, vision, and values of the company? Despite one's best intentions, I don't think so. This is why companies have coaches: so that we can constantly distinguish what is driving our behavior out of alignment with the rest of these circles, and how to shift back into alignment.

By *leadership effectiveness* I simply mean embodying the five Smart-Tribe Accelerators, which we covered in detail in part 2.

As we mentioned in chapter 4, it's essential that our team lives our company's *mission, vision, and values*, which means leadership must model them and reinforce them constantly. If the behaviors of an organization's leaders are not aligned with its values, you'll often first see anger and resentment, and then apathy, in team members.

We find some people may not be able to become profoundly aligned with other people, but they can and will become profoundly aligned with a potent mission, vision, and values.

As for the fourth component, *organizational effectiveness*, we'll need to drill down a little more deeply.

What Makes Organizations Truly Effective

First of all, if an organization is to be truly effective, it must at heart be a *learning organization*, a term that was coined by Peter Senge. A learning organization is a company that facilitates the ongoing education and development of its members and continuously transforms itself. A learning organization has five main features:

- **Systems thinking:** An understanding that all parts affect the whole and changes in any one part will likewise affect the whole. The best way to solve problems is to understand each problem in relation to the overall ecosystem and whole of the company.
- **Personal mastery:** The commitment by the individuals at the company to the process of ongoing learning and development
- **Mental models:** Willingness to challenge internal theories, norms, behaviors, and values
- **Shared vision:** A shared vision motivates the staff to learn, as

it creates a common identity that creates focus and energy for learning. The most successful visions build on the individual visions of the team members / employees overall.

- **Team learning:** Teams that share their learning processes openly see the problem-solving capacity of the organization improve greatly. Open, communicative cultures will help ongoing dialogue and discussion grow faster.

A SmartTribe can exist only in a flexible culture where learning and communication are consistent, and leaders and team members increasingly embody the SmartTribe Accelerators.

The Organizational Effectiveness Pyramid

In addition to having the heart of a learning organization, an effective organization also develops according to a relatively predictable process. We've found that the effectiveness of an organization is dependent on six components, or layers, that build upon one another.

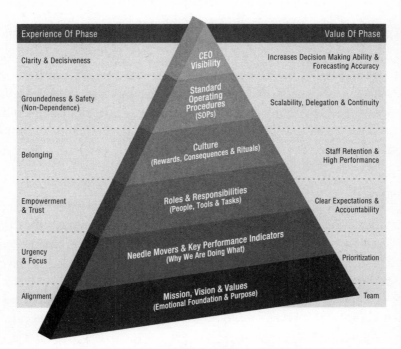

Figure 10-2. Organizational Effectiveness Pyramid

Mission, Vision, and Values

At the bottom is the emotional foundation and purpose of the organization, which is captured and communicated via the mission, vision, and values. It's a key component of both a sustainable SmartTribe as a whole and organizational effectiveness in particular. From this foundation, the team experiences alignment—we know why we're here, what we stand for, believe in, and hold sacred, and we know where we're going. Your mission, vision, and values will help you shift from offering your team merely a job to offering them a career and, ideally, a calling.

Needle Movers and Key Performance Indicators

This level of organizational effectiveness builds upon the emotional foundation and purpose of the mission, vision, and values because it directly supports why we are doing what. Since Needle Movers and performance tracking are covered extensively in chapter 5, I'll simply summarize here by noting that the best way for an organization to drive urgency, focus, and priority is in this level.

Roles and Responsibilities

When we're clear on the people, tools, and tasks we have available, and who "owns" what aspect of the business, we experience true empowerment and trust due to clear expectations and accountability. Empowerment without structure is anarchy. It defeats our purpose and all too often results in grossly overstaffed departments, divisions, and companies.

Culture

Having a solid culture fosters belonging, staff retention, and high performance. In chapter 5 we explored rewards and consequences, and in chapter 9 we worked on how to move through the logical levels of change to create the culture of our dreams. In chapters 11–14, you'll see examples of cultural rituals that deeply engaged and aligned team members.

Standard Operating Procedures (SOPs)

SOPs help us promote safety in our organization (since we don't have to depend on others for their help/knowledge) and reliability in that they remove mystery. We know the procedure, it's the one we rely on for quality and consistency, and we can ensure we'll get reliable results going forward. If you need assistance in creating SOPs, please refer to the kit in the Resources section below.

CEO (and Leader) Visibility

There's nothing like visibility to support clarity and decisiveness at the leadership level. When all the lower levels of the Organizational Effectiveness Pyramid are in place, leaders experience increased decision-making ability and forecasting accuracy. This of course boosts the top and bottom lines, as well as fostering safety, belonging, and mattering in the culture, since everyone knows where we're going, we're consistent in our strategy, we course-correct quickly, and everyone is contributing to the end result.

———

Do you see how each level of the Organizational Effectiveness Pyramid is supported by the SmartTribe Accelerators? Clarity supports the mission, vision, and values. Accountability supports Needle Movers. Focus and accountability support roles and responsibilities. Influence supports culture. Clarity and accountability support SOPs. And sustainable results support CEO visibility.

Now that you understand how the SmartTribe Accelerators work and the deeper process of organizational change required to create your own SmartTribe, let's up the ante with some more complex case studies. In the next four chapters, we'll see the SmartTribe Accelerators in action in four common business scenarios: getting leadership aligned with the culture overall; ending silos, sabotage, and system dysfunction; correcting when you've got the right person in the wrong role (and those unrelenting Untouchables); and how to conduct a talent turnaround. I chose these four cultural stuck spots because they are so common that you have likely come across them, and they are rich in learning opportunities. Since trouble often starts at the top, we'll launch into leadership and culture alignment first.

▼

Twitter Takeaways

Find these helpful? Tweet them to your tribe and reference #SmartTribes as the source. Thanks!

- The intersection of Behavior, Leadership Effectiveness, Mission/Vision/Values, and Organizational Effectiveness will determine the sustainable success of your SmartTribe.
- The Organizational Effectiveness Pyramid is your diagnostic tool to create an organization that supports your SmartTribe. The six levels are supported by the SmartTribe Accelerators.
- The best way for an organization to drive urgency, focus, and priority is via Needle Movers. Goals are often ineffective.
- Having a solid culture and compelling cultural rituals fosters safety, belonging, mattering, staff retention, and high performance.
- Want reliable results? Standard Operating Procedures help us promote independence, reliability, consistent quality, quick training, and they remove mystery!
- Visibility on company results supports clarity, increased decision-making ability, and forecasting accuracy at the leadership level. This of course boosts the top and bottom lines and morale since everyone is contributing to the end result.

Assess

- Which of the Four Factors of Sustainable SmartTribes are most powerful at your company? Which is the least?
    - Behavior
    - Leadership Effectiveness
    - Mission, Vision, and Values
    - Organizational Effectiveness

- Review the Organizational Effectiveness Pyramid. Which levels need work at your company?

- Mission, Vision, and Values
- Needle Mover and Key Performance Indicators
- Roles and Responsibilities
- Culture
- Standard Operating Procedures (SOPs)
- CEO (and Leader) Visibility

Act

- Per your Organizational Effectiveness check-in above: How would you prioritize the levels needing the most work? What SmartTribe Accelerators do you need to pay special attention to?
- For the "least" item(s) in the Four Factors of a Sustainable SmartTribe above, what are the greatest risks they currently pose? Who can help you mitigate these risks? How soon can you act to mitigate and then move toward removing them?

ROI

Applying the Four Factors of a Sustainable SmartTribe plus ensuring you have all the layers of the Organizational Effectiveness Pyramid done or in process will yield you the following ROI:

- Individuals will be 67–100% more emotionally engaged, loyal, accountable, and ownership-focused.
- Individuals will become 35–50% more productive.
- 3% will receive a promotion to a role with increased responsibility and management of others within six months of applying our techniques via coaching and training.
- 100% will increase their ability to significantly influence others and outcomes.
- 86% will report getting more done in less time due to the accountability techniques they will learn.
- 100% will report the ability to apply our communication techniques and thinking styles both at home and at work, resulting in an increase in personal fulfillment.

Resources

Helpful resources in this chapter include:

- Four Factors of a Sustainable SmartTribe
- Organizational Effectiveness Pyramid

Go to www.ChristineComaford.com/resources and download the kits that will be most helpful for you. We think the following kits would be a good start:

- Special Report: The Five Critical Mistakes That Halt CEOs
- Increasing Accountability and Ensuring Goals Are Met
- Leading from the Inside Out
- Managing Your Energy to Keep Your Momentum

Also check out the following in the appendix:

- Presence Process
- Seeking Balance via Connection

11.

SMARTTRIBE RX: LEADERSHIP AND CULTURE ALIGNMENT

s we discovered early on, the leaders set the tone for the entire culture. A focused and present leader creates a focused and present culture. Clear communication in the leadership ranks drives clear communication at all levels of the company, and so on. In this chapter, we're going to cover a particularly tricky stuck spot: Founderitis. It's tricky because the leaders with this affliction are often celebrated for their tremendous accomplishments. Yet the rise and the fall can be equally fast. Read on to learn how to identify, and cure, this insidious culture killer.

Jerry Yang is a smart, capable, visionary executive. So why did Yahoo! stock jump 4% when he resigned?

Founderitis. We've seen it before. We'll see it again. And for the record, I'm not immune to Founderitis. I've had it too. Severe reality distortion fields and misguided mergers are nothing new to me!

Cultural Stuck Spot: Founderitis

Founderitis is when the CEO is the source of the problem. We either have a cult of personality problem and/or the CEO is leading the company into dangerous territory. Here are the five warning signs of Founderitis:

1. Shunning a golden parachute for your shareholders (and yourself). When Yahoo! turned down Microsoft's acquisition offer a few years back, many of us were amazed. Their strategy was failing, their business was plummeting, and Microsoft was going to take their pain away and put $44.6 billion in their pockets in the process.

Why is this considered Founderitis and not a laudable attempt to reignite the company? The difference is in the denial factor—some might say delusional quality—of the response. The founder thinks his vision is better, he deserves a richer offer, or the acquirer isn't worthy of him. When competitors are pummeling you and you have no solid recovery strategy, it's best to cop to the fact that the party's over. No point in serving cocktails and celebrating your independence as the ship sinks.

2. Severe reality distortion field. We witnessed this with the 2011 botched Netflix price hike. Why hike the price? What's the justification? Where's the realistic connection with what the customer wants? "In hindsight, I slid into arrogance based upon past success," Reed Hastings said on his blog.[1] "We have done very well for a long time by steadily improving our service . . . [and promising to] work hard to regain your trust. We know it will not be overnight." Now, there's a CEO with courage—he'll recover from Founderitis.

3. Misguided mergers. Like really expensive designer clothes that are absolutely ugly, just because you can afford it doesn't mean you should buy it. When big companies acquire small companies, the Founderitis victim will do it out of boredom, fascination, obsession, jealousy, envy, and/or fear—essentially with no business case or the true desire to make $1 + 1 = 5$.

But mergers are tricky. After the glow of the press release, after the back slapping and champagne swilling is over, the fact is most mergers fail to meet their potential. Yahoo! buying Delicious and Flickr, News Corporation's acquisition of Myspace, Google's acquisition of Dodgeball, AOL's purchase of Bebo. The result? Promising companies with great potential and passionate users end up either shut down or marginalized. (Okay, just so I'm not a total party pooper, Amazon, Symantec, and Cisco have done a good job with some acquisitions.)

4. No care for the common folk. We saw this at Zynga in 2011–2012. People matter. Easily 80% of the real work is done by your team behind the scenes. The flashy deals the executive forges need to be implemented by someone. And who might that be? Oops—the people that the founder doesn't talk to? The people without a career path, working inhumane hours, and being told they're not delivering enough value? Hey! Way to motivate!

5. Rogue founder-CEO. We see this a lot in companies that blasted through the first few inflection points but don't yet have a strong C-suite. During a Cultural Assessment, a high percentage of team members (including managers) will have stories about the founder-CEO micromanaging and creating chaos. People don't take real responsibility or initiative because they know the founder-CEO will come along and change things anyway—or they are waiting for approval on nonstrategic business since there are no departmental budgets.

One company we worked with also had the not-uncommon problem of no executive protocol or rules of engagement, so C-suite members did not respond to e-mails, texts, calls, or other types of requests in a timely fashion. With no sense of urgency, low accountability in the culture was common—and so was low collaboration and camaraderie. Promises were made but follow-up often did not occur. Such as in the case where a key team member was offered a promotion by his boss, HR wasn't told, and the team member skulked around for six months terrified that he had done something wrong to lose the promotion, not knowing what and yet feeling unable to ask in the oppressive culture.

Realigning and Reinvigorating Leadership and Culture

When companies grow quickly, they often sail through the first few inflection points. Then they reach a critical mass of sorts, and the stagnation begins.

One e-mail I received contained the most worrisome Leadership Effectiveness Assessment I had ever seen. It was from John, CEO of Company AA, and he wanted help. *Now.* Here's how our conversation went:

"Christine, I've had it. Nobody does anything—or at least anything right—unless I tell them what to do. We need more engineers, but we can't find qualified people. I have no time for anything; I'm not sleeping. We grew really quickly in the first ten years of operation—we hit $177 million two years ago—but revenue was down last year, and this year we're still going to be below $160 million. Can you help?"

"It all depends on you, John." And that's the hardest part. If a leader comes to me wanting to work on themselves as they work on their company, then great. But if they think it's only their people that are the problem, I'm outta there.

John and I started coaching right away, and he quickly agreed to have me and my team fly out and do a Cultural Assessment (see sample questions in the Act section below). We had to know what was going on from the perspective of the team.

Would it surprise you to learn how little of John's challenge he could see? The results of the Cultural Assessment sent him into a tailspin. He thought he had a good culture and we would just need to "fix" a particular executive (who actually turned out to be great, but did need to be reallocated), restructure for more innovation, help him delegate a bit better, and he'd be on his way. To be fair, the company had grown rapidly and it had a stellar reputation. John was an excellent business builder and had created outstanding customer relationships. But John wasn't seeing the full picture of his culture's stuck spot.

Following his initial cry for help, John had swung a bit in the other direction, and by the time the Cultural Assessment was complete he had become a bit defensive. This is normal; we see it all the time. It takes a lot of courage to ask someone else to look under the hood and let them ask your team all kinds of intimate questions. All those things that look so grim when clumped together—each and every one of them—had a very good reason why they were the way they were. Safety. Belonging. Mattering.

Assess: What We Found

In sum, we found the dread disease of Founderitis. John's occasional micromanagement left executives irritated and employees felt there was no care for the "common folk"—team members described themselves as "the little people." The Reality Distortion Field was pretty intense too; the company often did not consistently listen to customer feedback. One product problem could have been resolved three years and hundreds of thousands of dollars earlier had the company listened to the customer and prioritized the resolution appropriately.

For each of the following case studies, we'll track each company with a SmartTribe Accelerator scorecard, so you can map the presence or absence of the SmartTribe Accelerators we covered in part 2: focus, clarity, accountability, influence, and sustainable results. Here's the scorecard for John's company:

SmartTribe Accelerator Scorecard

Focused. The entire company was ignoring the fact that they were in trouble. The CEO—and therefore the entire team—failed to add up the list, and they thought they were doing great. If they compared themselves to their competition, they were way ahead of the game, but guess what. Their competition was not a good barometer.

Clear. The company vision was active but misunderstood, and not a useful motivator. Team members dreaded Monday mornings because they knew the CEO would have been working over the weekend and their inboxes would be full of "sh#t-o-grams." The lack of explicit budgets created micromanaging.

Accountable. Without appropriate structures, accountability was inconsistent at best. The word *deadline* had no internal meaning, though there was the occasional mad scramble to satisfy a customer. The company lacked SOPs between sites, leading to work repetition and varying quality in executed assignments. The lack of an executive code of conduct led to unreturned calls, late or no e-mail responses, and unfulfilled promises, leading to lack of cohesion at the highest level of the company.

Influential. What was great fun about Company AA was that they were *so close* to having a great culture. All that was necessary was to add a little training and structure so they could use their influencing skills to keep everyone in their frontal lobes and increase their client rapport.

Sustainable Results. Revenue was inconsistent. Company AA had been swirling around the same inflection point for years. What they didn't know was that you are either going up or you're going down. So if you have ceased going up, it's only a matter of time before gravity grabs you.

Act: Here's What We Did

Company AA did not so much need a new set of vision, mission, and values statements as it needed to communicate the existing statement differently. Team members were familiar with it, but it was not having the desired emotional response. So when we implemented the new IDPs (Individual Development Plans), Needle Movers, and incentive plans, managers were trained to have a discussion with their direct reports about how their personal IDP, their Needle Movers, and their results contributed to the overall mission, vision, and values of the company.

The C-suite also started to put some skin into the game. They created a confidential endgame plan. They knew exactly what inflection point to achieve and how to get there, and when they got there, they planned to cash out of the business. Each member of the team had his or her own motivation to get there. John started to get a lot more pushback on his occasional forays into micromanagement from his team, whose future was explicitly at stake, and healthy conflict became a cultural norm.

Next, we launched the Cultural Assessment, where we worked to uncover what was not working for the team company-wide and create a plan to help John secure the support of the entire staff, the executive team, and the board.

We asked a sampling of the employee base as well as the executive team a series of questions, including:

- What is it like to work here now?
- What frustrates you the most?
- What motivates you the most?
- How do you feel about your role and responsibilities?
- If you could wave a magic wand and have the culture be any way you want, what would that be like?
- For members of the executive team: What motivates your team the most?

- For employees not on the executive team: How would you describe the executive team's leadership style?

Simply interviewing the team won't move the needle. Interviewing, assessing, creating and executing a plan, and generating results are key.

Here's how we increased and improved communication and culture. First, we instituted town hall meetings in which a brief company update was provided, a vision for the year and quarter was reinforced, team members were celebrated, and a twenty-minute education session was provided. The town hall ended with a Q&A session in which anonymous questions could be submitted in advance. No topic was off-limits. A culture of candor with kindness was developed as a result, and safety, belonging, and mattering were increased.

John and his executive team started asking tons of questions—focusing on five inquiries for each tendency to advocate (see chapter 3). This helped reduce order giving and taking.

Then, hooray! A People Plan was created to develop the current and future leaders. It contained the following:

- Individual Development Plans (IDPs)
- Leadership Development Programs (with us)
- Lean training (see the essential courses we recommend in the Leading from the Inside Out kit in the Resources section)
- Accountability structures and explicit rewards/consequences
- Departmental vision statements—mini versions of the company mission, vision, and values so that people knew exactly how their department fit in before working on their own Needle Movers

We provided executive coaching (the Map-enhancing techniques so they could get out of their own way, plus business strategy) to John and five of the key executives. We worked closely with both John and his VP of talent, Sally, to redeploy one executive and restructure another department.

Simultaneously, we coached Sally through a talent intensive (where we identify and launch the top three programs or processes to achieve HR objectives) and trained all managers in creating Needle Movers and career paths (IDPs) for the entire team, all three locations, and all of their 917 employees. All managers were trained in setting Needle Movers, tracking them weekly, and applying rewards and consequences. This initiative plus new communication protocols, real departmental budgets, and redesign of meeting structures meant that the company became a high-accountability culture within about six months. We created a Rock Star of the Month program, relocated a few offices and cubes to bring together some team members who were temporarily assigned to a technical implementation project, applied Meta Programs to streamline the recruiting process, and even threw a few parties to bring fun back into the place. As I'm sure you know, culture doesn't change overnight, and Company AA had to continue its focus and commitment over time to create true believers.

Simultaneously we tackled sales. We revamped the bonus and incentive structure to focus on more profitable products. We consulted with the sales and marketing teams on specific rapport and influence (see chapters 7 and 8) and custom messaging for prospects and clients alike.

Then came the Leadership Development Program (LDP, a six-month leadership development program of one-on-one coaching and training) and the Leadership Round Table (LRT, a six-month program similar to the LDP but with group coaching). These two transformative programs—the LDP for managers and high-potential team members who we think will soon be managers, and the LRT for nonmanagerial high contributors and influencers—brought the changes deep into the DNA of the company. Here's where the culture shifted from order takers in a low-accountability chaotic culture to highly motivated performers applying the SmartTribe Accelerators, as well as understanding and owning the organizational change as described in chapter 9. For details on what is involved in each of these programs see the Leading from the Inside Out kit listed in the Resources section.

We're still doing LDPs and LRTs at Company AA. We run two or three of each every year. And that's where the best news comes in: Company AA now has great employee retention of key players. They recently commissioned an employee satisfaction survey from a neutral party, and scores were through the roof!

ROI: What Company AA Got

The result? Revenue targets projected for two years later were achieved within twelve months. As of this writing, the company has successfully sailed through the $250 million inflection point and is on track for the $500 million inflection point in five years (or less, depending on the outcome of a potential acquisition). Here are the numbers for the first year of results:

- Increased CEO and key executive strategic/high-value time by ten to fifteen hours per week.
- Increased gross revenue by 44%.
- Shortened the sales cycle by 39%.
- Increased accountability and team performance by 61%.
- Increased marketing demand generation by 82%.

Twitter Takeaways

Find these helpful? Tweet them to your tribe and reference #SmartTribes as the source. Thanks!

- Companies can grow only as fast as their systems allow them to.
- Getting into the Smart State is about trust, and trust happens from consistent implementation.
- A focused and present leader creates a focused and present culture. Clear communication in the leadership ranks drives clear communication at all levels of the company.
- Do you know the five warning signs of Founderitis? Severe reality distortion field and no care for the common folks are the two most dangerous.
- Without appropriate structures, accountability will be inconsistent at best. The word *deadline* will have no internal meaning, work will be repeated, quality and execution will vary.

- Is your exec team as aligned as a rowing team? If not, add an executive code of conduct.
- Ask your team: What is it like to work here now? What frustrates you the most? What motivates you the most?
- Ask your team: How do you feel about your role and responsibilities? If you could wave a magic wand and have the culture be any way you want, what would that be like?

Exercise: Do You Have Founderitis?

1. When approached by or approaching a merger or acquisition (from either side), do you consider it calmly and choose your response?
2. Does your team have a systematic way to seek and get real-time customer feedback? Does your team make a habit of understanding market needs, wants, trends, and preferences? What gets done about it?
3. How do team members rate the company? Do they think they are working at one of the best places in the world?
4. Does everyone, from the CEO to the new intern, practice accountability?

Resources

If you answered no more than once in the exercise above, you may have Founderitis. Go to www.ChristineComaford.com/resources and download the kits that will be most helpful for you. We think the following kits would be a good start:

- Leading from the Inside Out
- Assess Your Team's Performance
- Knowing What You Want and How to Get There: Why Are You Building This Company?
- What Do You Stand For? Defining Personal Values
- Increasing Accountability and Ensuring Goals Are Met

Also check out the following in the appendix:

- Presence Process
- Needle Mover Worksheet
- Energy Recall

12.

SMARTTRIBE RX: ENDING SILOS, SABOTAGE, AND SYSTEM DYSFUNCTION

When an organization's people spend a bit too much time in their Critter State, we often see three troublesome symptoms: silos, or isolated departments that withhold information or collaboration from outsiders; sabotage, where departments or individuals try to prevent another's success, due to fear; and system dysfunction, where the proverbial right hand doesn't know what the left is doing and inefficiencies abound. There are two cultural stuck spots that we find particularly contribute to a Critter State–driven, fear-laden atmosphere where silos, sabotage, and system dysfunction rule: Deer in the Headlights and Old School. In this chapter we'll explore both, because we often see them together. Why? Both are often vision-related. In both cases the leadership team is blindsided because they either didn't look ahead and prepare for changes in the marketplace, so now they're stunned into inaction, or they got fat and happy and figured they'd ride it out. In both cases, leadership wasn't being present to what would move the company forward and now it's time to repair the damage.

But wait—there's more. Once everyone realizes they've been blindsided, the Critter State fear kicks in—and the tendency is to protect one's turf at any cost. So walls are erected or fortified, defenses are strengthened, and communication is dramatically reduced because it's every person or team for themselves. And the backstabbing begins (or continues). In scenarios like this, trust is *toast*.

Cultural Stuck Spot: Deer in the Headlights

Deer in the Headlights culture happens when a company not only hits an inflection point but its market also significantly changes. Not only are you coping with having to change everything internally but lots of external change has occurred too. Yet in this stuck spot, the Critter State response is to freeze. "Let's just pretend nothing is happening and carry on."

The CEO who stays in this spot without an aggressive plan or who refuses to take a bold strategic move ends up risking and possibly losing everything. This is often a case of a CEO operating from his own personal Stuck State and the company—as a reflection of him—following suit.

Let's have a look at AOL. This company was once way ahead of the game. Today the company is anemically surviving, with their most reliable revenue from dial-up customers who appear to be mostly more than sixty years old. We all gave up on their having a turnaround strategy after several failed attempts. Now, postacquisition, AOL is Microsoft's problem.

Compare this to IBM. In the late 1970s, IBM was primarily in the mainframe business. They were losing revenue and share price was dropping. Then in the early 1980s, they went into PCs and consulting. This required great risk, profound leadership (especially that of Lou Gerstner, who arrived in the early 1990s), and monumental culture change. Remember the OS/2 debacle in the early 1990s? They rose up and made it through that huge culture change again. Never give up on IBM: they may have moments of Deer in the Headlights, but they always find their way forward.

Cultural Stuck Spot: Old School

"We've always done it that way." "No one gets fired here." The response to every proposed solution is "We tried that once in 1987 and it didn't work." These are the refrains of a company whose stuck spot is Old School. What's wrong with Old School? If it ain't broke, don't fix it, right?

What's wrong is that an Old School company cannot meet the changes the market needs—and the market is constantly changing.

The difference between an Old School stuck spot and a Deer in the Headlights stuck spot is mainly about time. Old School companies are not as panicked because the pace of change is slow enough to give them the illusion of external safety. Old School companies have entrenched behavior patterns, and in terms of the Critter State fight/flight/freeze response to threat, they are fighting to keep things the way they are. This is how both situations create and foster silos, sabotage, and system dysfunction.

Ending Silos, Sabotage, and System Dysfunction

The two founders of Company BB were at war. The CEO was aggressive, the CTO often sabotaged the CEO, and the company was divided into two camps. In addition to their personal strife, there had been recent technological breakthroughs that were changing the way customers worked and put their product at risk of being obsolete.

Productivity across the organization was plummeting, and the executives didn't trust one another and didn't cooperate with one another. All the CTO wants to work on is strategy, but he's afraid he'll lose whatever power he has if he shifts to a new role and lets go of his direct reports. Further, because the culture is low on communication and high on fear, the COO has set up her own camp, and the CRO thinks all the executives except the CEO are "impossible" to work with. The silos are spreading.

- Meta Programs of the CEO: **Toward, Options,** External, General-Specific, **Active,** Sameness with Exception
- Meta Programs of the CTO: **Away, Procedures,** Internal-External, General-Specific, **Reflective,** Sameness with Exception

Note that we bolded the differences in their Meta Programs.

Assess: What We Found

Team members were dispirited. The feud at the top had not gone unnoticed and translated into turf wars, mixed loyalties, internal competition, and low motivation. When client projects were specified, the CTO's team and COO's team didn't talk, so the CRO was often livid when client deadlines were missed and projects were delivered with missing functionality.

In the early days, the company had revolutionized its industry, taking it out of the Dark Ages and into the twentieth century. The problem was that it is now the twenty-first century and their competitive advantage was eroding fast.

Their culture was stuck in Deer in the Headlights with some surprising (because the company was relatively young) elements of Old School and a touch of "right person, wrong role" from the next chapter to boot. They could no longer attract and keep the engineering staff they needed.

SmartTribe Accelerator Scorecard

Focused. This is a perfect example of a culture that had an outdated mission, vision, and values—the level of safety, belonging, and mattering was super low as a result. Plus there was extremely low communication. Since no communication rhythms existed, cross-team collaboration didn't happen, and no one had a stake in the success of another team.

Clear. Hidden or unexpressed conflict was rife throughout the company. Team members took the sabotaging behavior of the CTO as a cue and modeled this behavior, adding to the hidden agendas. Managers had all kinds of implicit expectations and no budgets or formal planning procedure.

Accountable. This was a classic low-accountability culture that needed to be transformed. Structures that support accountability, like IDPs to give team members a career path and SOPs for transferring information between departments, were either nonexistent or ineffective.

Influential. No one was truly connecting between teams, and influence was cultivated and cared about only within a given team. Collaboration was at an all-time low across the company. Blame was the norm between teams, as well as hiding or withholding key information.

Sustainable Results. The company was crumbling under the weight of the emotional stress of the executive team. Win-lose agreements were the norm, and burnout (after working woefully few hours) was increasing. People simply couldn't take working in such a guarded and hostile environment.

Act: What We Did

The CEO needed to help the CTO move into a new role before anything could happen. This was a priority to recover from Deer in the Headlights and Old School stuck spots because we badly needed his talents to be focused on creating a new strategic direction for the company.

We helped the CEO learn to speak in the CTO's Meta Programs to help shift him out of his Critter State. The CEO used this messaging to start the CTO's shift into his Smart State: "I need your help [give CTO power, enroll emotionally]. We're crafting a new strategic direction and I know we'll be growing really fast. I'm concerned that we'll move too quickly without mitigating the risks or taking the time to properly create the foundations to ultimately move even faster [Away, Reflective]. We need a step-by-step [Procedures] implementation plan to ensure we're ready for the growth that's coming, and I need someone who knows how to do this [Internal]. Few people here can see both the forest and the trees [General-Specific] like you can. You'd mentioned that you want to shift to a more strategic role and free up your time from management work. With a role like this you'd be doing what you're great at [External] and have the hassle of management work gone [Sameness with Exception]."

We helped the CTO get very clear on what he wanted (no direct reports and work on strategy only across departments) as well as set up office hours to avoid the constant interruption that made him crazy. We coached him to replace his sabotaging behavior toward the CEO with the influencing skills we covered in chapters 6 and 7. The CTO changed roles to become chief systems architect, letting go of his direct reports and accepted reporting to the CEO with clear conditions that honored his priorities. He gave up his seat on the company's board, creating an opening for an industry influencer to be added.

The CEO and new chief systems architect hashed out and communicated a new vision that team members owned and were inspired by. You can find the same tools we used to craft meaningful mission, vision, and values statements in the Leading From the Inside Out kit in the Resources below. That act alone created the same kind of motivational buzz that they had experienced in their early years—and they had created it *together.*

The stage was now set to bring up the rest of the team. This involved reducing the number of direct reports to the CEO partially through internal promotion and in one case through recruitment. We coached the entire C-suite on clarity of communication and got them using the tools for explicit communication in chapter 4.

Next, we guided (through both training and intensive coaching) the C-suite and senior management team through the process of creating new accountability structures (see chapter 5) using the tools in our Increasing Accountability and Ensuring Goals Are Met, Optimize Your Operations: Standard Operating Procedures to Streamline Your Operations, and Leading from the Inside Out kits (see the Resources section) to get on track.

They received intensive skills training in the SmartTribe Accelerators. In particular, they learned how to move from problem thinking to outcome thinking (chapter 8) and how to develop rapport using Meta Programs (chapter 6–7). By making all the changes structural rather than symptomatic, this team was able to turn their ship around and create sustainable growth.

Once the cultural change had been structured at the top, we began intensive Leadership Development Programs (LDPs) for their emerging leaders and company-wide Leadership Effectiveness training to make the SmartTribe accelerators part of the company's DNA. The LDPs were crucial to bringing up the next generation of innovators.

One critical factor to making collaboration more seamless and comfortable among previously disenfranchised team members was the use of social technologies. We followed Vala Afshar's ten steps to build a social enterprise and get everyone communicating more easily.[1]

ROI: What Company BB Got

The CEO of Company BB used coaching to help him gain back ten hours a week and improve his relationships, both personal and professional.

The new chief systems architect (the former CTO) is now adding huge strategic value as he and the CEO work together to orchestrate the next industry revolution. The two of them double-date with their spouses once per month to ensure maintenance of their easy, warm friendship.

Company BB was able to make their new strategic direction profitable quickly as it capitalized on existing assets and they accelerated through the $250 million inflection point at which they had been stuck. About one year later, they sold off an unprofitable part of their business and regrouped under the guidance of the realigned CEO and chief systems architect. Then they secured funding for their next surge. The culture had a few hiccups at the time of that change, and we were brought back in to help. With renewed intention and training, they are now accelerating toward the $500 million mark.

------------------------▼------------------------

Twitter Takeaways

Find these helpful? Tweet them to your tribe and reference #SmartTribes as the source. Thanks!

- Deer in the Headlights culture happens when a company not only hits an inflection point but its market also significantly changes. The Critter State response is to freeze and pretend nothing is happening.
- Old School cultures have missed the bus but have the illusion of external safety. They have entrenched behavior patterns and are fighting to keep things the way they are. This creates silos, sabotage, and system dysfunction.
- Silos, sabotage, and system dysfunction are symptoms of lack of cultural alignment.
- Successfully and continuously adapting to market forces has to involve deep, engaging, and explicit work on core values.
- Rolling out a new strategic direction benefits from skills training for all team members.

Exercises

Are You the Deer in the Headlights?

This is probably the hardest one to own up to, so I'll ask only a few questions:

1. Has your target market expanded and/or do you see new markets you could address as well?
2. Do you have confidence in your plan to address market conditions and opportunities?
3. Has revenue continued on an upward trend, with profit increasing as well?

Are You Old School?

1. Do your executives stay current with the latest leadership techniques and quote key customers and/or current business leaders?
2. Is "fail fast" part of the company mantra?
3. Do team members feel like their ideas get fair consideration? Do you know?

Resources

If you answered no to more than one question in the Deer in the Headlights exercise or in the Old School exercise, go to www.ChristineComaford.com/resources and download the kits that will be most helpful for you. We think the following kits would be a good start:

- Funding Is Only Half the Battle: Funding and Founder Fundamentals
- Special Report: The Five Critical Mistakes That Halt CEOs
- Increasing Accountability and Ensuring Goals Are Met
- Leading from the Inside Out
- Managing Your Energy to Keep Your Momentum

Also check out the following in the appendix:

- Silence Practice Techniques
- Energy Recall
- Seeking Balance via Connection

13.

SMARTTRIBE RX: RIGHT PERSON, WRONG ROLE

Have you ever worked for a company where priorities were constantly shifting, where employee turnover was high and trust was low? Then you know all about Chaos Culture. When a culture is in perpetual chaos we see hasty decisions made without due consideration because the Critter State is rampant.

Cultural Stuck Spot: Chaos

We worked with a company in Chaos Culture. The CEO asked our team to facilitate at a crisis meeting that summed up just how poor the company's culture had become. At the meeting another consultant was present too—one who was helping them with some long-range plans. Why was he present at the crisis mitigation meeting? No idea. His work had nothing to do with the challenge at hand and it was distracting.

One team member had invested considerable time and energy in the long-range plan and had not been clearly told that there even was a major crisis and that we were meeting to work through it. He was understandably disoriented and felt devalued.

During the meeting, we had to constantly bring the team back on track to solve the crisis. One team member managed to stay focused and thus was given most of the responsibility for implementing the solution. Within a month, she quit out of sheer frustration, crisis unresolved.

And on and on.

Chaos Culture means not seeing the forest for the trees.

Right Person, Wrong Role (Plus Naming Untouchables)

More often we see Chaos Culture play out because roles are not clearly defined or we have the right people—great people—doing the wrong thing. The more people are mismatched or unclear about their roles, the more chaos we find in the organization or in that particular part of the company.

People get into the wrong roles for any number of reasons. Perhaps there was a reorganization and the company didn't want to lose them so they were reallocated without consultation or training. Maybe they were promoted beyond their capability without a training plan or they were hired to do one project that has since become irrelevant and the company is not tapping their huge potential to produce meaningful results elsewhere. And then there's our all-time favorite, the Untouchable.

Do you have Untouchables? These are people who were hired because they are related to (or friends with) the CEO or other team members and thus may have been (over)promoted or allowed to stay on for emotional reasons.

The real problem with "right person, wrong role" is how to correct it and still have a culture of safety, belonging, and mattering. Some may be reporting to a manager who feels threatened by the "bright spark" passing them on the organization chart, and in some cases we have to get much more present with what is actually happening and much more clear about where we are going (our mission, vision, and values) before we know how to use the person appropriately. It's also key to determine if someone is indeed a "right" or a "wrong" person. A right person is generally talented and simply needs to be put in the right role. A wrong person doesn't match or honor the organization's values, or does but doesn't uphold the leadership code of conduct. Sometimes we just have to let go and let people move on, knowing that ultimately it's better for everyone.

Here's a case where we found Chaos Culture and had to do a little of all of the above.

Company CC was a tech consulting firm with $37 million in annual revenue and approximately 270 employees, about two-thirds of whom were consultants. They were tracking at $137,000 in *revenue* per employee . . . ouch!

The company was run by a couple, John and Sarah, who initially contacted us about perfecting their sales process. They felt that their salespeople could be performing much better. What we found was a much bigger issue.

Assess: What We Found

The findings were grim: a fear-driven culture with 53% employee turnover each year. Company CC did an exceptional job of technical training for new hires—only to see them leave for higher pay within a year.

The two owners of the company had virtually opposite Meta Programs, and this was causing chaos. Sarah (Active, Toward, Options, Difference) would proactively start an initiative, rally the troops to move toward the new goal, then jump to the next option/project. John (Reflective, Away, Procedures, Sameness) would want to analyze before launching the new initiative, so he would kill it or block it, minimize exposure, and set up a procedure to handle the proposal through testing—no matter how much or little the cost or associated risk. The resulting chaos was confusing the team and sending them deep into their Critter State.

The glaring gap in the consultants' training curriculum was in sales. Even though their role was heavily client-facing, the consultants weren't trained in basic selling skills and had no incentive to do anything but fix technical problems. They also had no interaction with the sales team—which was sequestered in a different area of the building. The consultants were the right people in the right role—but with no support to perform their best.

Harry, the new sales manager, had been with the firm for three months. Shortly after hiring Harry, the company had reorganized to close a failing business unit and Sarah and John had moved their niece, Toni, the VP of the failed unit, into a new role as VP of sales and marketing. There were three problems with this scenario: (1) Harry had no sales expertise—his entire background was in Internet marketing; (2) Toni was an experienced sales manager but wasn't strategic and had no marketing expertise; (3) the two disliked each other—Toni was threatened by Harry, and Harry thought Toni should have been fired for her lackluster leadership of the failed business unit. To further the nepotism, Toni's boyfriend, Taylor, had been hired as director of client care. He had solid experience, but a perpetual mocking smirk when interacting with anyone but Toni.

SmartTribe Accelerator Scorecard

Focused. It was time for John and Sarah to address their organizational issues and determine the right people for each key role. They had denied the demotivation team members suffered by promoting their niece Toni in spite of her poor performance. It also was time to take a long hard look at how their relationship was affecting the company.

Clear. The company vision statement was a defense of their past: it read like a big excuse for what had gone wrong—and so it inspired no one. The company had some good SOPs but fostered cliques and political behavior due to favoritism demonstrated by both John and Sarah. Roles were not clearly defined, so often redundant work resulted.

Accountable. There were few consistent applications of accountability practices. People were fired but no one knew why. People were promoted but no one knew why. In sales, there was insufficient tracking of quotas, and the pipeline quality was questionable. No one in marketing was clearly accountable for demand generation or lead qualification.

Influential. With this much fear and this much chaos, it's not possible to be influential. Far from feeling empowered, people kept their heads down and tried to survive until they found another job.

Sustainable Results. Revenue was already declining. Team members were pressured into working long hours with no incentives. Turnover was increasing monthly. Panic was the norm and there were no cultural practices or support to move into their Smart State.

Act: What We Did

This culture was clearly in chaos. The first thing John and Sarah did was use our leadership kits (see Resources below) to create clear and compelling mission, vision, and values statements. This is key to ending chaos: you have to know what you stand for, why you're coming to work, and where you would like to go. The second critical factor is to tie your structures to that rigorously—remember to implement like a banshee to move through inflection points.

Ironically, this company's technology consulting practice was designed to make workplaces more fun, more exciting, and better-run places of business by providing technical tools, processes, and improved workflow. People were attracted to work at Company CC because of the impact of their work.

After digging in with the entire executive and senior management teams, we decided the benefits of their services should be the explicit values for the whole company, and the mission and vision became clear. They posted the new statements in the lobby, and the managers worked with their smaller teams until all team members knew how their department fit in.

We now had to help them work inside out in the logical levels of change (chapter 9)—from core/culture to environment—to make sure all parts were aligned. Together we established Needle Movers (first for the executive team and later for everyone) in line with the new mission, vision, and values, and radically increased accountability using weekly reporting and energetic application of the Accountability Equation (chapter 5).

More specifically, we created a reporting process for the sales pipeline (see Resources below for our Streamlining Your Sales Funnel kit to help you qualify leads) and marketing effectiveness metrics (see Resources below for our Marketing Optimization and Focus kit), and set up an incentive plan for the consultants to source future sales.

We also redefined the roles and responsibilities throughout sales and marketing to get the right people in the right roles. Some people were reallocated, and one or two were let go. The layoffs were especially tricky since the company had a history of high employee turnover and we wanted to convey that this move was different. Since the foundations had been set through the highly visible mission, vision, and values project and Needle Mover implementation, the clarity of communications around the changes was well received and served to diminish rather than increase the Critter State.

Next, the leadership team learned the five SmartTribe Accelerators so they could get in and stay in their Smart State and help their teams do this as well. They learned how to build a culture where Victims, Rescuers, and Persecutors were transformed into their positive alternatives, as you learned in chapter 8. They dived into learning how to influence outcomes and increase connection through the rapport and Meta Program tools (in chapters 7 and 8).

John, Sarah, Toni, and Harry were each coached individually to work on their own key challenges. Toni got the tools to turn her department around. Harry was moved out of sales management and into the right role, marketing, where he is brilliant and a perpetual learner. He still reports to Toni, who now manages the sales team directly. Harry's initiatives have made Company CC top of mind in their target market. Now that John and Sarah communicate more explicitly, they are no longer creating chaos, and Toni and Harry have developed mutual respect for each other. Taylor had to be let go. He didn't want to uphold the company values, and had burned too many bridges to be salvageable.

The entire consulting group learned the influencing and rapport techniques (see chapters 6 and 7) so that they could communicate more effectively with clients, and we worked together on their common challenges in potential sales scenarios. A new incentive program rewards the consultants for supporting sales. They now work regularly with the sales team to develop accounts.

In a second phase, the whole company—each and every team member—created Individual Development Plans (IDPs; see Resources for the Leading from the Inside Out kit for an IDP template), so everyone now has a career path. This has added a further boost to motivation and engagement, and has ultimately led to a much higher employee retention rate.

ROI: What Company CC Got

About six months into the change process, things got pretty scary. The consultants became resistant and didn't want to work on internal projects for which they had no billable hours, and John and Sarah almost pulled the plug and reverted to chaos. Instead they applied the energy management tools they had learned (see chapter 9), worked through their own resistance, recommitted, and held their team accountable to the direction they had chosen together. The results were not all immediate—patterns occasionally resurfaced and had to be re-addressed—but overall in our years together the results have been phenomenal. They zoomed through the $50 million inflection point and are preparing for $100 million. Their employee retention is now normal for their industry, and employee surveys show that engagement and satisfaction are steadily getting better.

As for the right team member formerly in the wrong role: Harry attributes his success to Toni's training efforts, while Toni attributes hers to Harry's marketing savvy.

Twitter Takeaways

Find these helpful? Tweet them to your tribe and reference #Smart-Tribes as the source. Thanks!

- "Chaos" culture results in hasty decisions made without due consideration because the Critter State is rampant. Often here we have the right people in the wrong roles.
- A "right person" is talented and needs to be put in the right role. A "wrong person" doesn't match or honor the organization's values or does but doesn't uphold the leadership code of conduct.
- To end chaos: know what you stand for, why you're coming to work, and where you would like to go. Then tie your accountability structures to this rigorously.
- Build a culture where Victims, Rescuers, and Persecutors are transformed into their positive alternatives.
- Chaos is an indication that you need to go back to basics. Start by reestablishing your mission, vision, and values, then line up your systems.
- Great people in the wrong roles is a sure symptom of Chaos Culture. Once you've got your systems lined up with your core values, do an audit and make sure the people you love also love their work.

Exercise: Are You Contributing to Chaos?

1. When you set corporate and team priorities, do they stick and stay until the priority is completed?
2. Is your employee turnover rate low? If it is high, what is causing the turnover and how can you reduce it?
3. Are your business results competitive? Are you tracking to a clear growth plan?

Resources

If you answered no more than once in the exercise above, you may have a Chaos Culture. Go to www.ChristineComaford.com/resources and download the kits that will be most helpful for you. We think the following kits would be a good start:

- Marketing Optimization and Focus
- Streamlining Your Sales Funnel
- Leading from the Inside Out
- Increasing Accountability and Ensuring Goals Are Met
- Assess Your Team's Performance
- The Ultimate Recruiting Kit
- Optimize Your Daily Operations: Standard Operating Procedures to Streamline Your Operations

Also check out the following in the appendix:

- Values Exercise
- Needle Mover Worksheet
- Seeking Balance via Connection

14.

SMARTTRIBE RX: TALENT TURNAROUND

What happens when our previously emotionally engaged employees start to become the source of our biggest problems? This is the time to look in the mirror and figure out how their spirits became crushed. Turning around talent, bringing them back to their positive and high-performing Smart State, is our job as leaders.

But talent is only one aspect of execution. Sometimes, if you can't get the right people, you need to go back and adjust expectations on the strategy. Per the 2012 PricewaterhouseCoopers CEO survey we mentioned in chapter 1, 24% of the CEOs reported, "We cancelled or delayed a key strategic initiative" due to talent constraints.[1] Ouch.

If you ever wondered about the ROI of knowledge management and collaboration, ask yourself about the strategy-execution feedback loop and how developing open and transparent dialogue, access to content, and informed decision making would benefit both those who set strategy and those responsible for executing it. You may have a cost model for project execution, but do you really know what it costs, and what it takes, to execute strategy? Something to ponder.

In this chapter we'll tackle a common stuck spot that we often see in larger companies: Crushed Culture. This stuck spot, like all the others, affects all levels of leadership and team members overall. The most challenging part of it is the low energy/low enthusiasm/despondency we generally see. As you'll recall from chapter 9, we want emotion to move change forward. So with Crushed Culture we often work on stimulating resistance or mockery or any other energy in order to counteract the apathy.

Cultural Stuck Spot: Crushed Culture

It's a disease. And it's going to become an epidemic if we don't do something about it.

As evidence, I offer three companies I used to love (which are strong, recognizable brands but shall here remain nameless) that now have Crushed Culture. It's spreading. It may not be immediately visible in stock prices or revenue, but in an age when customers are freely advertising their complaints on the Internet and social media (and their peers are listening), it will be only a matter of time.

Here are the three warning signs of Crushed Culture:

1. Employees no longer care about the customer's experience. My favorite eyeglass shop, a national chain, lost a pair of my frames. They said, "Bummer," and dismissed me. The counter guy practically looked right past me and asked how he could help the next person in line. One popular airline carrier used to have great service. On a four-hour flight we were offered water only once. When I went to the galley to get something to drink, the flight attendants scowled at me.

2. Maintenance is out the window, and commitments are not honored. I used to frequent a particular hotel chain because I knew I'd have a consistent brand experience. The rooms would be clean, well-maintained, and safe, and the lobby would be lovely. At this hotel in Midtown Manhattan my room had two walls with peeling wallpaper (yes, it hung off in four-inch strips!) and my wake-up call never came.

3. Team members become order takers with little initiative or accountability. I recently had a run-in with customer service at a major communications company. She repeated what she thought she had been instructed to say five times—yes, I counted. Her script had very little to do with my problem, and I began to wonder if her ears were painted on. I finally had to ask to speak to a supervisor. If she were being rewarded for solving problems, she could easily have solved mine or bumped it up to a supervisor using her own initiative and without waiting for my frustration level to exceed her indifference. She's probably a nice person, but she's working at a company that is holding her in her Critter State.

Crushed Culture will easily stall a company at an inflection point.

Contrast the above experiences with a company like Zappos, which blew the doors off online customer service simply by empowering people to solve problems. They're focused on creating a culture that fosters prefrontal-lobe thinking—and it works.

According to the fall 2011 Gallup Poll on employee engagement,[2] 71% of American workers are "not engaged" or are "actively disengaged" in their work, meaning they are emotionally disconnected from their workplaces and are less likely to be productive.

Wow. And this trend has remained stable for 2010 and 2011. Word is the 2012 numbers will be the same.

Does this concern you?

And don't think Crushed Culture symptoms are in the rank and file alone.

"Our team is full of order takers."

"Why do we have so little accountability around here?"

"We're going through a lot of change. Why don't our people embrace it?"

These are but a few of the most common complaints and concerns I often hear from the C-suite. And I've been listening for a long time. Employee disengagement, or Crushed Culture, has spread to the C-suite too.

Talent Turnaround: When Good People Have Bad Attitudes

We all know that to accelerate through inflection points, to create a SmartTribe, it's first and foremost about people. Many stuck spots are caused by common problems in the area of talent management—or lack thereof. Your head of talent (or HR, if you call it that) needs to be an integral part of your C-suite team and should be seen as a strategic asset.

Sometimes the problem is that you already have great people but you've let them languish. When we understand our universal, subterranean need for safety, belonging, and mattering, then we can also understand quite quickly how letting people languish is asking for emotional disengagement and bad attitudes.

Company DD is a large payment-processing-equipment company. Their biggest customers are nationwide retail chains. When we first began working with them, they had not had a new product in two years and were relying on increasingly anemic sales to long-term customers.

Assess: What We Found

Cost cutting had been the principal focus for a revolving door of CEOs, all guns for hire, who had had little incentive to do anything but what the board asked them to do: increase profit by cutting costs. The new CEO was different: he had successfully cut some costs, but he knew that if the company was to stay in business, they needed to change—and fast.

When we performed the Cultural Assessment, morale was at an all-time low. Managers with R&D or engineering responsibilities routinely squashed ideas. The few IDPs that existed had little to no relevance to a team member's day-to-day experience and had been created ages ago, then stuck in file cabinets, never to be referenced again. Whatever talent they had was trapped by a Crushed Culture.

SmartTribe Accelerator Scorecard

Focused. The CEO needed to recognize a number of things in order to create an action plan that would move the needle. The death of the founder and CEO a few years previously had never been grieved, and the rotating interim CEOs inflicting half-hearted initiatives had seriously impacted company spirit and loyalties. The company also had little in the way of IDPs and had difficulty attracting and retaining key engineering talent.

Clear. The company's vision, mission, and values were out of date and unemotional. They hung on the wall of the entry hall, covered in dust. While the CEO knew they had to create new products or die, there was no credible action plan to get there and an unclear sense of where the market opportunities really lay. The company had become rather detached from its customers.

Accountable. It was virtually impossible to be fired from this company. With few or no IDPs, no cultural value of accountability, and no incentive plans or measured goals and objectives for innovation or product development (only cost, quality, and safety targets), the company was not designed to grow.

Influence. The top of the organization was classic Industrial Revolution structure. If someone didn't report to you, it was assumed you could not influence them. It was very difficult to get real information from anyone if it was not produced automatically by existing, out-of-date structures.

Sustainable Results. Revenue was already declining. Key team members had left or were planning to leave. The situation was highly unstable.

Act: What We Did

We coached the CEO to craft new mission, vision, and values statements with his executive team within the first ninety days of working together. The new statements were far from ideal, but they were owned by the senior management team, had some emotional impact, and were at least alive. They were great platforms from which to progress, and they could easily be communicated throughout the company.

The senior management team also defined more aggressive revenue goals for new markets and customers. They began to actively support and drive their external sales agents.

We began primarily by coaching the C-suite. They needed to implement IDPs and a new bonus and incentive scheme, one that clearly rewarded customer-driven behavior, gave engineers incentives to persevere with new ideas, and rewarded innovative ideas and implementation for everyone from factory floor to administrative staff to management. It is important to note that many of these rewards and incentives were not monetary; they had to do with public recognition, training, and career advancement—the things that turned out to be most important to the team.

After the first three months, we began rolling out training for the management team. They were being asked to switch from Old School style to SmartTribe style, and by this point in the change process they were well into the resistance phase of the Organizational Change Adoption Path—the perfect time to acquire some new skills. This was also perfect timing to create common language for all team members, as the new incentive plans and IDPs were then being rolled out. We relied extensively on the techniques from chapter 9 to help them shift their identity and manage deep levels of cultural change.

Next, we worked with the talent team to create two innovation programs: an Innovation Incubator Team (IIT) and Innovation of the Month (IOM). There are three critical factors to implementing each of these programs. First, they must allow people to critique ideas. New evidence has shown that the old "suspend all critiques" brainstorming framework sounded right but didn't work in practice.[3] Second, next actions and action owners have to be defined by the end of the meeting, and there must be high accountability on those items. Third, such programs need to be massively supported from above so that the initiatives don't happen once or twice and then fade away.

Innovation Incubator Team. The company needed structured brainstorming with cross-functional teams in order to innovate better and faster. Creating an Innovation Incubator Team would get innovation top of mind and ensure that new products had diverse champions. Here's how it worked. First they selected a variety of expertise and perspectives for their IIT: representation from sales, engineering, manufacturing, client care, marketing, and finance. They set a regular date for this two-hour brainstorming meeting, with everyone bringing an idea for a new product innovation. Each innovation had a projected ROI, an owner to drive it to completion, and a cross-functional team to support it.

At the close of each IIT meeting, the owners of the innovations that were approved would specify deliverables and deadlines for their innovation to keep momentum. Then they'd update the IIT on weekly progress via social technologies like the company blog or simply basic e-mail status reports.

Innovation of the Month. Since Company DD wanted innovation to occur anywhere in the company, they created an Innovation of the Month program, complete with rewards and celebrations (see chapter 5 on accountability). Team members submit their ideas by completing a form on the corporate intranet. They include any diagrams or supporting materials with their application. The Innovation of the Week has:

- Category (product, service, process)
- Expected ROI (to be tracked over the next ninety days)
- Details of the innovation (what it is, why, who is affected by it and is needed to create it)

An innovation can be as simple as the bookkeeper reducing a bill-paying process by three steps and thus saving five minutes per bill to an entirely new product line to an improvement to a current product to a new high-margin service. The IOM is selected by a three-person cross-functional team, and the winner is celebrated on the Innovation Wall of Fame, where each innovation is summarized with a photo of the innovator. The innovator is acknowledged and appreciated publicly via the company newsletter, the CEO's blog, and company meetings, and gets a certificate to hang in their office (cheesy, yes; cute, yes!) plus a twenty-five-dollar Starbucks card.

After the ninety-day ROI period is over, and the company knows what the ROI of the innovation truly is, the prize gets bigger. From the IOM winners, an Innovation of the Quarter winner is selected based on ROI and positive impact on the company.

Company DD recently launched its new Leadership Development Program and they are a little more than six months into working through our program. Experience has shown us that this is when the change will become permanent. When all levels of management are trained and have the SmartTribe Accelerator practices in their DNA, the SmartTribe culture achieves critical mass and begins to accelerate all processes.

ROI: What Company DD Got

The CEO became aware of some personal changes he had to make in order to become a SmartTribe leader and, with coaching and some Map-enhancing techniques (see chapter 6), has been able to make those changes. He has moved from sitting in his ivory tower fretting about Company DD and not knowing the names of the majority of the employees to actively walking around and engaging with his team.

Company DD shifted from a declining revenue stream to gaining more than 8% revenue growth within the first 120 days. This result was mostly thanks to the sales team, who quickly embraced the rapport and Meta Program techniques in chapters 6 and 7. Using these new tools they rapidly engaged existing customers to place new or expanded orders. The CEO backed all of these efforts powerfully, in many cases jumping on airplanes at short notice to help close a deal. The trust and camaraderie across the company was increasing, with safety, belonging, and mattering being demonstrated daily.

In the first ninety days of the Innovation of the Month program, fifteen process, product, or service innovations were submitted from four of the eight company departments. Wow.

Within the first 180 days, team member morale had improved by 23% as measured by quarterly Net Promoter Score (NPS) surveys. The company recently went on a recruiting spree and has been able to attract and retain key engineering staff.

―――――――――――▼―――――――――――

Twitter Takeaways

Find these helpful? Tweet them to your tribe and reference #SmartTribes as the source. Thanks!

- You may have a cost model for project execution, but do you really know what it costs, and what it takes, to execute strategy?
- Does your team have low energy / low enthusiasm / despondency? You may have "Crushed Culture."
- Signs of Crushed Culture: employees don't care about clients, commitments are not honored, employees become order takers with low initiative/accountability.
- When we understand our universal need for safety, belonging, mattering, we understand quickly how letting people languish is asking for emotional disengagement and bad attitudes.
- Do you have an Innovation Incubator Team (IIT) and Innovation of the Month (IOM)? If not, start now to harness the creativity of your team, get them deeply engaged, boost revenue.

- Your innovation incubator needs a cross-functional team, tight directive, lively brainstorming, healthy conflict, and relentless follow-through.
- For each proposed innovation track: category (product, service, process), expected ROI (to be tracked over the next ninety days), details (what it is, why, who is affected by it and is needed to create it).

Exercise: Do You Have Crushed Culture?

1. Are your team members highly accountable?
2. Do they have a "Thank God It's Monday" attitude?
3. Do they take initiative and often have new ideas and innovative approaches?
4. Do they get frequent appreciation and public acknowledgment?

Resources

If you answered no more than once in the exercise above, you may have a Crushed Culture. Go to www.ChristineComaford.com/resources and download the kits that will be most helpful for you. We think the following kits would be a good start:

- Leading from the Inside Out
- Assess Your Team's Performance
- The Ultimate Recruiting Kit

Also check out the following in the appendix:

- Presence Process
- Needle Mover Worksheet
- Seeking Balance via Connection

15.

SUMMARY
How to Measure Your SmartTribe ROI

Wow—what a journey we've taken together. Now let's sum it all up so you can move forward in creating your own SmartTribe. You now have five SmartTribe Accelerators (focus, clarity, accountability, influence, and sustainable results) and their corresponding tools to help you and your team move from your Critter State to your Smart State. You have diagrams and charts to use when explaining these concepts to your team, and you can even have them enlarged to post in your office (see the appendix to contact us for this). And you know how the Accelerators support your organization's growth too. Fantastic work—thanks for sticking with me!

Now let's look at some real-world scenarios you may be facing right now so we can preempt any challenges that could slow you down.

Quick Reference Chart for Solutions to Common Business Challenges

After getting this far, you probably already have an idea of where you are and where you'd like to be. But let's talk about situations that might already (or may tomorrow) have you in your Critter State and how to quickly snap back into your Smart State. Below are some common business and communication challenges that can potentially get you or your team members stuck, and the tools you'll want to reference to move through these stuck spots.

You also might want to revisit table 2-1 in chapter 2 ("Behaviors That Send Us into Our Critter State and Smart State") for some ways we guide our team into a given state based on our communication. It's a challenge to help your team become a SmartTribe, but ultimately it's absolutely crucial for your business—and even the teams most stuck in the mud can find their way out using the SmartTribe Accelerators.

Challenge	Tools and location
Overwhelm: too much to do, focus challenges	Three dimensions of focus (chapter 3), high-value vs. low-value activities, accountability structures (chapter 5), Energy Allocation Chart (chapter 8), tension to empowerment (chapter 8)
Controlling: resisting delegation	Safety/belonging/mattering (chapter 2), inquiry versus advocacy (chapter 3), clarity of plan (chapter 4), three change processes (chapter 9)
Delivering bad news: layoffs, terminations	Tension to empowerment (chapter 8), change processes (chapter 9)
Giving problematic performance feedback; conflict management and resolution	Three-chair exercise (chapter 4), Outcome Frame and rapport tools (chapter 6), Meta Programs (chapter 7), tension to empowerment and energy allocation (chapter 8)
Motivating someone to take on more, rise up	Accountability structures (chapter 5), Outcome Frame and rapport tools (chapter 6), Meta Programs (chapter 7)
Communicating consequences	Three domains of clarity (chapter 4), four levels of consequences (chapter 5), change processes (chapter 9)
Change messaging: incentive plans, new initiatives, new responsibilities, new strategies	Safety/belonging/mattering (chapter 2), Meta Programs (chapter 7), change processes (chapter 9), case studies (chapters 11-14)
Rallying the troops: public speaking at company and team meetings	Safety/belonging/mattering (chapter 2), mission/vision/values and three domains of clarity (chapter 4), rapport tools (chapter 6), Meta Programs (chapter 7)
Marketing: messages not sticking, lead generation low, team needs plan and process	Focus tools (chapter 3), clarity of plan (chapter 4), inquiry versus advocacy (chapter 3), Outcome Frame and rapport tools (chapter 6)
Sales: reluctant prospect/unhappy client	Safety/belonging/mattering (chapter 2), Maps and rapport tools (chapter 6), Meta Programs (chapter 7), sustainability tools (chapter 8)
Product development: low innovation/output or low enthusiasm	Accountability structures (chapter 5), case studies (chapters 11-14), change process (chapter 9), Outcome Frame and rapport tools (chapter 6)

Here's one final scenario where you'll see how the tools and techniques presented in this book were applied with solid success for a struggling organization:

When I spoke with the COO of a leading technology company on Wednesday morning, Hudson had already been in thirteen meetings. No wonder he didn't have enough strategic time—thirteen meetings (totaling twenty hours) in 2.25 days was de rigueur at his company. What was happening in all those meetings? I had to find out. After a series of questions, it was clear: Hudson and his team spent too much time info sharing and getting new hires up to speed—requiring dozens of people's precious time.

The intention was good (making sure everyone knew what was up, getting new hires looped in); it was just that the execution was too expensive. We had a communication and visibility problem, and to make matters a bit more complex, I learned that the company didn't use to have excessive meetings. After acquiring a competitor, they had struggled through a rough integration process. Some key players on the "sell side" had objected to the merger, and some key "buy side" players had objected to the acquisition. Emotions were high, the Critter State was rampant, and the C-suite had decided to increase communication at any cost.

First, it was key to smooth out the bad feelings. We performed a Cultural Assessment for the company and 360 Assessments of the entire executive team. Now we knew what the exact issues were, and we got to work. Next Hudson and his extended management team were trained on the SmartTribe Accelerators. Now that everyone was focused and present to the communication improvement opportunity—which was primarily a safety, belonging, and mattering issue—they swiftly streamlined meetings and reduced the number of people involved. Info sharing is now done via e-mail forty-eight business hours before a meeting. Meetings across the company have been reduced by more than 50%, and are 50–75% shorter. All leaders know that when a person displays challenging behavior, it's time to look for whether they want more safety, belonging, or mattering, use the Outcome Frame to learn what they seek (chapter 5), and then deliver this support via speaking in the person's Meta Programs (chapter 7).

The result is that 388 leaders just gained more than 4,268 hours *each week*. Now they have enough time to work on key strategic initiatives and high-value activities. And the best part? Reaching their division's $1 billion inflection point within two years is no longer a fantasy.

Although you're working on making your whole team stronger, interpersonal relationships are key as well. Sometimes one team member will require additional coaxing to get them into their Smart State and on board with where the entire team wants to go.

Here's a quick process I'll often use when working through an interpersonal communication challenge:

1. Determine the outcome I'd like by using the first three questions of the Outcome Frame (What would you like? What will having that do for you? When will you know you have it?).
2. Do the three-chair exercise (see chapter 4) to step onto the Map of the person I will be communicating with. This also helps to reveal their Meta Programs in the problem context.
3. List the person's Meta Programs in the problem context and craft a message (see many examples in chapter 7).
4. Choose the best influencing phrase (see chapter 8) to kick off my communication.
5. Book a thirty- to sixty-minute (depending on the complexity of the situation) meeting with the person so we will be uninterrupted and have privacy.
6. Deliver communication and work together to find a solution.

Determining Your Metrics of Success

My initial promise to you was the high ROI of a SmartTribe. I'm a bit fanatical in making sure that each and every one of our clients gets the results they want. Our clients choose which metrics are important to them and we track them together, so we always know exactly how much gross revenue, net profit, or profit per employee has increased— or how much undesired employee turnover, cost of sales, or number of executive hours spent on low-value activities has decreased. What's so satisfying, or what Steve Jobs would call "insanely great," is the clear relationship between investing in people and gaining tangible results and ROI. This is why I want you to choose your success metrics soon.

Let's start small. We find repeatedly that ROI on coaching is tied to either behavior change (for example, inquiring instead of order giving, releasing judgment and condemnation of team members, or collaborating with other departments in very specific ways) or achieving company initiatives (see the below metrics). Coaching ROI should be at least twenty times the money invested annually. Company-wide ROI should be the same—at least twenty times the return in value delivered. What will move the needle for you? That's what you'll want to measure.

Once you start addressing your stuck spots and begin creating your SmartTribe you'll likely find that some parts of your organization aren't working as well as you had thought. Grab your Inflection Point chart (figure 1-3 in chapter 1). Do you need a Sales Assessment? A Marketing Assessment? An Execution Assessment? Is it time for a 360 Assessment or Cultural Assessment? You'll find some of the most popular ROI metrics our clients like in the appendix.

Yes, the investment in creating a SmartTribe takes time, energy, funds, and heart. But some forms of ROI can take as little as 90–180 days:

- Individuals become 35–50% more productive.
- Marketing demand generation increases by 31–237%.
- Marketing messages are 37–301% more effective.
- Individuals are 30–73% more emotionally engaged, loyal, accountable, and ownership-focused.
- 97% tangibly contribute to increasing key executive strategic/high-value time by five to fifteen hours per week.
- 100% increase their ability to significantly influence others and outcomes.
- 86% report getting more done in less time due to the accountability techniques they learned.
- 100% report the ability to apply our communication techniques and thinking styles both at home and at work, resulting in an increase in personal fulfillment.

And other forms of ROI can take one or more years:

- Revenues and profits increase by up to 210%.
- Sales are closed 22–50% faster.

- New products and services are created 29–48% faster.
- Sales close rate is increased by 44%+.
- 63% receive a promotion to a role with increased responsibility and management of others within six months of applying our techniques via coaching and training.

We know that whatever you've committed to track, you've also committed to grow. Companies large and small have gone before you on this journey. They've had rough days when they were firmly stuck in their Critter State. Then they tapped into their SmartTribe tools and shifted both themselves and their teams into the Smart State. Please know I'll be with you every step of the way. Together we're creating more safety, belonging, and mattering in the workplace. Congratulations—you are already on your way. We also find that if you follow our process, you'll realize your ROI faster.

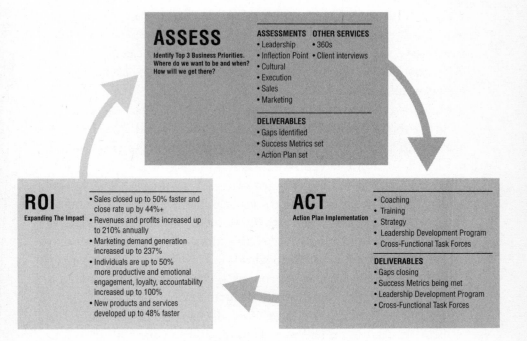

Figure 15-1. CCA's Three-Step Process

See how this works? We follow the Assess step above in parts 1 and 2 of this book. Then from there we complete the process, create an action plan, implement it, and then enjoy the ROI and results. At each stage, we have deliverables to keep the momentum and energy high. When your SmartTribe is a reality, you can expect high safety, belonging, and mattering, which means your team's reward network will be lit up. Problems will be skipped or solved smarter and faster. When someone slides into their Critter State, a team member will help them shift back to their Smart State, with compassion and possibly even humor. Communication will be open and honest and nondefensive. And people will love where they work—which will boost both the top and bottom lines, and significantly increase talent retention and the ease of recruiting.

Positive Target Fixation

Before we part I want to leave you with one last practice that members of a SmartTribe use to keep themselves focused or to get unstuck. Years ago, I took surfing lessons in Maui. My instructor had me positioned in a terrific location, except it was near a jetty made of rocks. As a nice wave would begin to build, I'd paddle hard to catch it and my instructor would yell, "Watch out for the jetty!" Needless to say, I'd surf right into it.

He didn't know about positive target fixation.

So I explained the concept and asked him to yell, "Surf to the beach!" And I did. Beautifully, consistently, because that was where I focused. Where you look matters.

Wayne Dyer shared a cool quote with me a few years back: "When you change the way you look at things, the things you look at change." When you want to buy a new car, you suddenly see it everywhere. Did that particular make, model, and color suddenly appear on the road in droves? Nope. You just changed what you looked at.

What are you looking at? If you get in your Critter State and you look at what is not working, what is so hard, you're practicing negative target fixation, and your brain will find all the reasons why things are so difficult. Your brain will work hard to validate your reality.

Yet if you ask, "Why is it so easy?" you'll fixate on a positive target. For example: "Why is it so easy to streamline our sales process?"

"Why is it so easy to find the perfect [new hire role] for our company?" "Why is it so easy to create marketing messages that resonate deeply?" You get the idea. Try it. It's fun, it's free, and it'll snap you right into your Smart State.

If you have questions as you grow your SmartTribe, please let me know—I'd love to help. If you have ideas and best practices from creating your SmartTribe, please share them! We'd love to hear from you at the following sites:

> SmartTribe Twitter community: #SmartTribe
>
> Twitter: @comaford
>
> LinkedIn: www.linkedin.com/in/comaford
>
> Facebook: www.facebook.com/comaford
>
> Phone: 415-320-6580
>
> Website: www.ChristineComaford.com

Let's keep the momentum moving. Let's keep fostering safety, belonging, and mattering in the workplace and all other scenarios. Let's help everyone we interact with to get in and stay in their Smart State. Thanks for the opportunity to be of service to you, and thanks for joining me on this adventure. Here's to your SmartTribe!

Twitter Takeaways

Find these helpful? Tweet them to your tribe and reference #SmartTribes as the source. Thanks!

- Do you feel overwhelmed, stuck, irritable? You're likely in your Critter State. Join the discussion to get out of it now!
- What would you like? What will having that do for you? When will you know you have it?
- How do you measure ROI on developing leaders? Our clients see gross revenue, net profit, or profit per employee has in-

creased and undesired employee turnover, cost of sales, number of executive hours spent on low-value activities has decreased.

- Coaching ROI should be at least twenty times the money invested annually. Company-wide ROI should be the same—at least twenty times the return in value delivered.
- Assess, Act, then see the ROI—this process works GREAT!
- When in your Critter State you look at what is not working, what is so hard, and your brain will find all the reasons why things are so difficult. Your brain will work hard to validate your reality.
- When you ask, "Why is it so easy?" you'll fixate on a positive target. "Why is it so easy to streamline our sales process?" "Why is it so easy to find the perfect [new hire role] for our company?" It's fun, it's free, and it'll snap you right into your Smart State.

ACKNOWLEDGMENTS

This book is the result of countless hours from people committed to bringing these tools to the world. First, my writing team of Janet Schieferdecker (a key member of the Christine Comaford Associates team), and Amanda Rooker. Janet played a huge role in helping me to shape the book, get the structure right, assist in writing it, and keep me in my Smart State during the process. Amanda helped refine, organize, edit, and optimize it. Her editing brilliance is unparalleled. I couldn't have created this book without these two exceptional women. Period.

The amazing team at Christine Comaford Associates—Alexis Chapman, Barbara Milo, Kathryn Turconi, Paul Keetch, Volker Frank, Jessica Randolph—provided support in the book refinement, website and social media work, back office, and details in general. Thanks to Kane Minkus, former CCA team member, and thanks to Dottie DeHart, our fabulous publicist, for helping us get the word out. I appreciate you all so much!

Thanks to my agent, Jim Levine, of Levine Greenberg, who kept asking me to refine what I wanted to say until we reached a level of clarity that resonated. Thanks to David Hancock, Lyza Poulin, and Jim Howard at Morgan James for helping to create our preview version of this book. Adrian Zackheim and Niki Papadopoulos at Portfolio championed *SmartTribes*, while Natalie Horbachevsky provided an editorial review that all authors dream of: thorough, thoughtful, and tremendously helpful. Thanks for making *SmartTribes* a better book, Natalie. Will Weisser and his team provided the book marketing genius—thanks, gang!

To our amazing preview readers, Vala Afshar, Jason Beans, Eric Brevig, Scott Eisenberg, Michael Krigsman, Amanda Marshall-Rock, Daniel Newman, Stuart Newton, Rick Thompson, and Mark Urban—

thanks for your generosity. Michael McNett, MD, and Howard Rankin, PhD, were terrific medical sounding boards. I know you are all tremendously busy and your feedback made a huge positive difference! I owe you one.

To the brilliant neuroscientists and cognitive science researchers at UCLA, Carnegie Mellon, Columbia, NYU, Stanford, and the NeuroLeadership Institute, thanks for providing the research to support our real-world results.

Now to the personal thanks. Geoff Heron, my amazing husband, has been a supporter through thick and thin. I didn't know my life could be so amazing until he showed up. My tribe of friends who are always ready to tell me when I am nuts, when I need to work less, when I need to play more—Marina McMillan, Michele Ikemire, Christine Crandell, Peg Videtta, Bonnie Digrius, Paul Vela, Michelle Miller, Theresa Teuma—you are the best friends a woman could ever have. My mom, Nancy Comaford, has supported my many career and creative endeavors too—thanks, Mom! My mentors who keep me in line and call me on my "stuff" include Jerry Jampolsky, Diane Cirincione, don Oscar Miro-Quesada, Carl Buchheit, Jeff Schmitt, Bonnie Knezo, Judy Hoaglund, the nineteen hospice patients I have had the honor to support in their final days—teachers all. Thanks for sharing your wisdom and helping me to remember what matters.

In my thirty-five years of studying personal development and human potential, several organizations and techniques have been, and continue to be, exceptional. The Center for Attitudinal Healing, the Hoffman Institute and its director, Raz Ingrasci, NLP Marin, Erhard Seminars Training (now known as Landmark Education), Hospice by the Bay, Napa Valley Hospice, Neuro-Linguistic Programming, cognitive behavioral therapy, transactional analysis, and the world's largest religions. And thanks to the monks who had me clean toilets for two days straight in order to prepare me to serve the Dalai Lama. There's nothing like cleaning toilets for remembering we all have one unit of self-worth—no more, no less.

To have Marshall Goldsmith, a fellow executive coach I greatly admire, write the foreword for my book was a huge boon. Thanks to Marshall and his terrific assistant, Sarah McArthur.

And last, to the thousands of people I've met in my travels and at my speeches and had the great good fortune to work with briefly or for prolonged periods of time, especially our courageous and committed clients: you have made all this work worthwhile. Every day you remind me that our time on this gorgeous and mysterious planet is fleeting, and there's no time like now. So let's be in our Smart State!

ABOUT THE AUTHOR

Bill Gates calls her "super-high bandwidth." Bill Clinton has thanked her for "fostering American entrepreneurship." *Newsweek* says, "By reputation, Christine is the person you want to partner with."

For more than thirty years, *New York Times* best-selling author Christine Comaford has been helping leaders navigate growth and change. She is best known for helping her clients create predictable revenue, deeply engaged and passionate teams, and highly profitable growth. She delivers these impactful outcomes as a result of her decades of building her own and her clients' businesses, plus her expertise in human behavior and applied neuroscience.

Christine is sought after for providing proven strategies to shift executive behavior to create more positive outcomes, enroll and align teams in times of change, and massively increase sales, product offerings, and company value. Her coaching, consulting, and strategies have created hundreds of millions of dollars in new revenue and value for her clients. The potent neuroscience techniques she teaches are easy to learn and immediately applicable to help leaders see into their blind spots, expand their vision, and more effectively influence outcomes.

As an entrepreneur, Christine has built and sold 5 of her own businesses with an average 700% return on investment, served as a board director or in-the-trenches adviser to 36 start-ups, and invested in more than 200 start-ups (including Google) as a venture capitalist or angel investor. Christine has consulted to the White House (Clinton and Bush), 700 of the Fortune 1000, and more than 300 small businesses. She has helped more than 50 of her clients exit their businesses for $12–425 million. Christine has repeatedly identified and championed key trends and technologies years before market acceptance. She has also been a software engineer at Microsoft, Apple, Adobe, and Lotus.

Christine has been called to serve two U.S. presidents in managing change. She worked with the Clinton administration on developing and implementing the U.S. intranet strategy, which ultimately enabled millions of Americans to access government services through the Internet. Under the George W. Bush administration, Christine helped to reinvent the Small Business Administration and pass a $4 billion bill in Congress.

Christine has also led many unconventional lives, adding to her 360-degree ability to understand business not just as a set of strategies but also as a complex web of human interaction. Her triumphs and disasters are revealed in her *New York Times* (and *USA Today, Wall Street Journal, Businessweek,* and Amazon.com) best-selling business book *Rules for Renegades: How to Make More Money, Rock Your Career, and Revel in Your Individuality* (www.RulesForRenegades.com).

Christine is a leadership columnist for Forbes.com. She has appeared on *Good Morning America, The Big Idea with Donny Deutsch,* CNN, CNBC, MSNBC, FOX Business Network, PBS, and CNET, and is frequently quoted in the business, technology, and general press at large. The Stanford Graduate School of Business has done two case studies on her, and PBS has featured her in three specials (*Triumph of the Nerds, Nerds 2.0.1,* and *NerdTV*). CNET has broadcast two specials covering her unconventional rise to success as a woman with neither a high school diploma nor a college degree.

Christine believes we can do well and do good, using business as a path for personal development, wealth creation, and philanthropy.

For Christine's coaching and training to create your SmartTribe, please visit www.ChristineComaford.com/ or call her on 415-320-6580.

APPENDIX

In this section I'll provide additional tools and resources that will help you to implement the SmartTribe Accelerators. First we'll start with the pragmatic proof that your SmartTribe is a good investment by providing some of the ROI metrics our clients track for cost justification. We all want to have tons of energy in our lives, yet we often "burn up" our energy inefficiently or get drained via being stressed or disconnected to what deeply matters to us. Below I'll provide processes that will help you to get still, then "recall" your energy when you feel "empty," and, finally, reestablish what really matters so you stay more balanced going forward. Further, you'll find templates and processes to increase accountability and presence, and to get in touch with what truly matters to you in business and life.

• • •

ROI Metrics for Your SmartTribe

What are the best success metrics for your business? Here are some metrics that our clients track:

Leadership/Company-wide ROI Metrics

- Revenue growth (per month, quarter, year)
- Profit
- Net income
- Gross revenue/employee
- Net income/employee
- Effectiveness of leaders
- Hours worked, compensation
- Multiply gain by compensation/hour
- Increase in scores in Leadership Effectiveness Assessment[1]
- Measurable improvement in challenging behaviors from 360 Assessment results
- Percentage of time on high-value versus low-value activities
- Number of people in division or department promoted annually
- Valuation of company
- Intellectual property
- Strategic alliances
- Long-term recurring revenue
- Market leadership (tracked by www.klout.com and other sources)

ROI per Department

MARKETING
- Percentage conversion
- Percentage frequency of purchase
- Market reputation / thought leadership
- Percentage increase in marketing demand generation
- Percentage increase in quality of leads

SALES

- Percentage increase in size of qualified pipeline
- Percentage decrease in sales cycle
- Percentage decrease in sales close time
- Percentage increase in average transaction size
- Percentage increase in customer lifetime value

TALENT/HR

- Turnover—percentage voluntary and percentage involuntary, and for each:
  - Regretted percentage
  - Not regretted percentage
- Percentage decrease in time to hire, position fill percentage, percentage retention
- Percentage increase in employee delight (via Net Promoter Score or other survey method)

OPERATIONS

- Process streamlined by percentage
- Cost reduction percentage
- Workflow: time percentage improvement
- Percentage reduction in staff hours / touches
- Efficiency/SOPs
- Inventory turn increase percentage

ENGINEERING

- Product delivered on time percentage
- Product delivered on budget percentage
- Product delivered at prestated quality percentage

FINANCE

- Percentage decrease in collections—DSO (days sales outstanding)
- Cost of capital

Presence Process

This process is from my Leading from the Inside Out kit. It is a ter-rific process for starting meetings or anytime you want everyone to become immediately present. For the complete kit, please download it from www.ChristineComaford.com/resources. Thanks to the Hoff-man Institute for the basic outline of this process. Modifications were made by CCA.

Start each meeting with the following Presence Process to foster safety, belonging, mattering:

- "Stand up tall and feel your feet on the floor. Feel your full height, stretching from the bottom of your feet to the top of your head. Feel your energy and solidity. Feel your dignity. Feel how present you are, right here and now."
- "Next feel your full width—the width of your feet, legs, torso, arms, chest, head. Feel the amount of space you occupy on the planet. You're supposed to be here. We're all so glad you're here with us."
- "Next feel your depth—feel from the front of your torso through the back of it. Feel where you are. Feel your purpose in life. Feel your commitment to yourself, your loved ones, your colleagues. Feel the difference you are making in the lives of the people you interact with."
- "Thanks for being present with us all today. Your being here matters. [Look at each person for a second to establish con-nection.] Okay, let's start the meeting."

Values Exercise

Thanks to Sharon Pira (www.SharonPira.com) for teaching me this process.

Description of Values

Values will remind you of who you are and what in your life is worth living for. Identifying your values is a process of discovery—a journey inward to who you really are. It is important that you understand that your Values Compass is only as accurate and effective as the accuracy of the values you identify.

By aligning your goals with your values and referring to them when faced with difficult decisions, the sense of struggle, overwhelm, and frustration in your life can virtually be eliminated. This *does* take time; however, living with a conscious awareness can unlock your true potential, in business and in your personal life.

Morals and Values Are Not the Same Thing

MORALS
- Decisions and judgments we make about what is right or wrong in our lives.
- Focused on our behavior, ethics, standards, and the principles we live by.
- Morals involve a conscious judgment or a decision-making process.

VALUES
- A value is intrinsic to who you really are.
- Define what is desirable for you to have in your life because it is who you are.
- Something you need, want, and *have to have* in order to make you smile, feel fulfilled, and feel like life is worth living.
- Values usually underlie our morals.

Step One

Think about a time in your life when things were very good. This would be a time when you were totally "at choice," the best time of your life. It can be a day, a period of time, a time when you were young, in high school, in college, or the present. Identify that time, write about it briefly, and write about the feelings associated with it for you.

Step Two

Look at the values list below and identify what words on the list were totally present for you during that time in your life.

Values List

Accomplishment/Achievement
Adventure
Clarity
Commitment
Community
Connecting/Bonding
Compassion
Creativity
Emotional Health
Environment
Excitement
Freedom
Fun
Harmony
Health
Honesty
Humor
Integrity
Internal Power

Intimacy
Joy
Leadership
Loyalty
Nurturing
One with Nature/Outdoors
Openness
Orderliness/Organization
Partnership
Personal Growth and Learning
Privacy/Solitude
Recognition
Romance/Magic
Security
Self-Expression
Sensuality
Service/Contribution
Spirituality
Trust

What values on the list were being totally honored during that time in your life that you just described?

Values Exercise

Thanks to Sharon Pira (www.SharonPira.com) for teaching me this process.

Description of Values

Values will remind you of who you are and what in your life is worth living for. Identifying your values is a process of discovery—a journey inward to who you really are. It is important that you understand that your Values Compass is only as accurate and effective as the accuracy of the values you identify.

By aligning your goals with your values and referring to them when faced with difficult decisions, the sense of struggle, overwhelm, and frustration in your life can virtually be eliminated. This *does* take time; however, living with a conscious awareness can unlock your true potential, in business and in your personal life.

Morals and Values Are Not the Same Thing

MORALS
- Decisions and judgments we make about what is right or wrong in our lives.
- Focused on our behavior, ethics, standards, and the principles we live by.
- Morals involve a conscious judgment or a decision-making process.

VALUES
- A value is intrinsic to who you really are.
- Define what is desirable for you to have in your life because it is who you are.
- Something you need, want, and *have to have* in order to make you smile, feel fulfilled, and feel like life is worth living.
- Values usually underlie our morals.

Step One

Think about a time in your life when things were very good. This would be a time when you were totally "at choice," the best time of your life. It can be a day, a period of time, a time when you were young, in high school, in college, or the present. Identify that time, write about it briefly, and write about the feelings associated with it for you.

Step Two

Look at the values list below and identify what words on the list were totally present for you during that time in your life.

Values List

Accomplishment/Achievement	Intimacy
Adventure	Joy
Clarity	Leadership
Commitment	Loyalty
Community	Nurturing
Connecting/Bonding	One with Nature/Outdoors
Compassion	Openness
Creativity	Orderliness/Organization
Emotional Health	Partnership
Environment	Personal Growth and Learning
Excitement	Privacy/Solitude
Freedom	Recognition
Fun	Romance/Magic
Harmony	Security
Health	Self-Expression
Honesty	Sensuality
Humor	Service/Contribution
Integrity	Spirituality
Internal Power	Trust

What values on the list were being totally honored during that time in your life that you just described?

Keep track by putting a check mark to the left of each word you identify.

Step Three

Think about one of the worst times in your life. This would be a time when you felt trapped, like you had no choices, a time when you were sort of at rock bottom. Identify that time, write about it briefly, and write down the feelings associated with it for you.

Step Four

Identify the words from the list that were NOT being honored for you during the time you described.

Which of these words were clearly not present for you during that time in your life?

Put an *X* to the **right** of the words you identify this time.

Step Five

First, for the statements below, fill in the blanks with words on the values list.

You can choose up to three words from the list for each statement. Write the three words on the blanks provided.

If _____ were missing from my life, I would be totally miserable.

_____

When I have _____ I feel peace and harmony with myself and the world around me.

_____

Step Six

Notice the values that kept showing up and make a new list of words that showed up more than twice. Use the following spaces to narrow your list of values. Feel free to add words that are not on the list. Write down the new list of words. Usually there are fifteen or less.

_____   _____
_____   _____
_____   _____
_____   _____
_____   _____
_____   _____
_____   _____

Step Seven

Start with the list you came up with and narrow it down to your top five. These are the top five values that you absolutely could not live without.

Write down your top five values in the blanks below:

_____
_____
_____
_____
_____

My request of you is:

Define in a short sentence what each of these top five words on your list means to you.

At least once a month, go to your top five values and rate yourself on a scale from one to ten on how well you are living those values right now, ten being very well and one being not at all.

Needle Mover Worksheet

TOP 3 NEEDLE MOVERS FOR THE YEAR

_____

_____

_____

Needle Mover #1:

Target:

Minimum:

Mind Blower:

What Needs to Happen to Achieve This Result:

Needle Mover #2:

Target:

Minimum:

Mind Blower:

What Needs to Happen to Achieve This Result:

Needle Mover #3:

Target:

Minimum:

Mind Blower:

What Needs to Happen to Achieve This Result:

TOP 3 NEEDLE MOVERS FOR THE MONTH OF_____

Needle Mover:

Target:

Minimum:

Mind Blower:

Needle Mover:

Target:

Minimum:

Mind Blower:

Needle Mover:

Target:

Minimum:

Mind Blower:

Silence Practice Techniques

When we stop our thoughts, we stop the world. Our thoughts are the voice of our ego, and our ego is primarily driven by fear. According to the research of Dr. Fred Luskin of Stanford University, a human being has approximately sixty thousand thoughts *per day*—and 90% of these are repetitive!

Just how much value can a repetitive thought add? Why do we have repetitive thoughts? Great questions. I believe we have repetitive thoughts because most of us haven't trained our minds to be still. Our minds and thoughts can be trained, you'll see results fairly quickly, and in stillness (or silence) you will find all of the answers you seek.

Here are some practices I've shared with countless people over the past few decades. To date, one of them has resonated with every person I've met. If you are the exception, let me know, and I'll submit more practices.

All of these practices are helpful for insomnia too. Simply do them in bed, as you are lying awake.

Prepractice Prep: Turn off all phones / noise makers. Ensure your family/colleagues/etc. cannot disturb you. Sit up straight, whether in a chair or cross-legged. You may want to set a timer for five minutes. If you simply do silence practice daily for only five minutes you will see and feel a difference in thirty days or less.

Practice: Heart Opening

Say "me" and touch your chest. If you do this a few times, you'll notice you always touch the same area. This is the position of your spiritual heart, or your heart center (or chakra).

Close your eyes. Place your inner focus on your heart center. See a rosebud there, choose whatever color you like. Now see the petals slowly unfolding in your heart center. This rosebud has an infinite number of petals. See them unfolding as the rose gets bigger and bigger, filling up your chest. Keep focusing on the rose unfolding.

When thoughts arise, let them pass, do not cling to them or reject them. Simply focus on the rose unfolding.

Practice: News Feed

Imagine a news feed across the bottom of a TV screen. There's a bit of news, then some white space, then more news, and so on. Your thoughts are like the news. There's always more! Now consider the white space between the thoughts. In Japanese, the word *ma* is loosely translated to mean "pause"—the pause between notes, the pause between breaths, the pause between sentences, the pause between thoughts.

Close your eyes. Place your inner focus on the constant stream of thoughts scrolling across the TV of your mind. See the scrolling thoughts floating in space or actually across a screen, whatever image works for you.

Don't pay attention to the thoughts in detail. Let them scroll by, neither cling to nor reject them. Now focus on the space between the thoughts, the *ma*, the pause. As you focus on the white space between the thoughts, you'll find it getting wider, longer, bigger. In time you'll see mostly emptiness, with few if any thoughts.

Focusing on *ma*, pause, emptiness, is a nice practice during the day too. Stop and notice open space as conversations pause, as music pauses. We are surrounded by pauses. That's where some of the best stuff is. We often fill our minds and schedules out of fear of emptiness. Yet emptiness is where true peace and connectedness and love can always be found.

Practice: Light Shower

Close your eyes. See yourself with your inner vision. You're sitting exactly where you are, dressed as you are. You are watching yourself. Move your focus to the top of your head. See a shower of white light pouring down over your head, covering your body gradually. Keep watching it pour over you as it covers you entirely, covers your outfit, your fingers, your face, your shoes or toes. It covers your front and back sides.

You can no longer distinguish your features; you simply see an image of you made of white light. This is the light of God, the Universe, whatever resonates with you. This light is always available to you; all you need to do is remember to tune in to the light shower.

When thoughts arise, let them pass, do not cling to them or reject them. Simply focus on the light shower covering you completely.

This is a terrific technique to do midday if you feel tired or upset.

Practice: Brain Dump

Back in the mainframe computing days a *core dump* was when the memory and all buffers were "dumped," or emptied. The result was pages and pages of gibberish as the buffers were flushed. Doing a core dump of your mind can be helpful when you have a constant swirl of thoughts.

Here's how to do it:

1. Get in a quiet place where you will not be disturbed. Turn off phones, etc. Have a piece of paper and a pen ready.
2. Light a candle and ask for the highest good for yourself and all beings.
3. Set a timer for twenty minutes.
4. Now start writing about any issue you are obsessing about, want to clear from your mind, want to understand or be free from, or have a question about. Just write, unedited and unpunctuated. When the sheet is full, turn it over, then upside down, then on its side, etc. You will not be reading this later, so there's no point in using more than one sheet of paper. The only purpose is to keep writing until the timer sounds.
5. When the time is up, either burn the paper or tear it up and flush it down the toilet. Wash your hands and change your physiology (jump up and down for a moment, roll your shoulders, etc.).

Energy Recall

This is a technique taught to me in many variations by several teachers, including BPI and Myra Lewin (www.halepule.com). I am grateful to them all.

We all place energy out in the world—in people, places, projects. We place energy generally in an attempt to get something accomplished (like in a key colleague to help them get a project done for us, or in our partner to get him or her to do what we want). Another time we place energy is when we have a negative judgment about someone—in that case we'll push our energy out to them to try to make them change.

The trouble is we often leave our energy where we placed it—even when its purpose is complete. Countless clients of ours have done this Energy Recall process only to find they still had energy in former coworkers from years ago!

Here's how it works.

Close your eyes. See a large golden sun about four feet above your head. This is your energy. Now in your mind's eye flick a switch and notice that the sun is now magnetic. Ask it to call back your energy from wherever you have placed it: in other people, physical locations, specific projects, maybe even your calendar. Many people see the energy coming back in disks, like pancakes or Frisbees; others see it as streaming energy or light. See it however you see it.

Regardless of the form the energy takes, track where it came from—where had you placed it? You can do this by "looking" at who is at the other end of the returning energy. If you see energy as a disk, flip the recalled energy disk over—can you see what is written on the back? Is it someone's name or a location or project? See the energy stream or disk rejoining your sun and merging back into it.

Once your energy is recalled, flip a switch on the sun and see the energy in the form of golden light pouring down into you and over you until you're solid golden light. Then see it radiating off you to your office, town, state, country, and the globe.

When you understand how much energy you are putting out and to whom, you will understand why you sometimes feel drained. Then you can work with your coach on putting energy into the positive alternative, the Relationship Bubble, which is the third part in each relationship—the "us." For every relationship, something is being created, the merger of the two people, the joint "project." When you put your energy there, and not directly into the person, you will not feel drained.

Seeking Balance via Connection

According to Dr. Edward Hallowell, an expert on anxiety and stress, there are twelve ways in which people need to connect in order to have full, rich, healthy, long lives. I had no idea how disconnected I actually was until I read his outstanding book, *Connect: 12 Vital Ties That Open Your Heart, Lengthen Your Life, and Deepen Your Soul*. I learned more about connecting in that book than I have from any shrink or at any seminar. Here's his list of where we should all be connecting, and the questions to ask for each.

Ask yourself these questions:

Family of Origin:

Do I have strong bonds and clear communication with my parents, siblings, relatives? Do I connect with them regularly?

What are some ways I might increase connection?

_____

Immediate Family:

Do I treat them with love and respect?

_____

Are we emotionally close?

_____

What are some ways I might increase connection?

_____

Friends, Neighbors, and Community:

Do I see friends and neighbors on a regular basis?

_____

Do I share my life with them frequently?

_____

Do I make time to enjoy their company?

_____

Am I involved in community groups and projects?

_____

Do I identify with and support the community I live in?

_____

What are some ways I might increase connection?

_____

Work Relationship:

Do I have emotional equity and a sense of mission at work?

_____

Do I share a connection with my coworkers and company?

_____

What are some ways I might increase connection?

_____

Appreciation of Beauty:

Do I enjoy beauty regularly—do I appreciate it and pay attention to it and savor it?

_____

Do I take time to enjoy a favorite art form?

_____

What are some ways I might increase connection?

_____

History and Human Legacy:

Do I feel part of the history of humankind?

_____

Do I learn about it, feel the power of it, and cherish the history of my country, town, culture?

_____

What are some ways I might increase connection?

_____

Nature and the Outdoors:

Do I connect with nature on a weekly basis?

_____

Do I spend time outdoors or indoors caring for plants or appreciating nature?

_____

Do I have special places that are healing to me?

_____

What are some ways I might increase connection?

_____

Pets and Animals:

Do I enjoy playing with and having a relationship with a pet?

_____

Do I value animals and enjoy seeing them, listening to them, interacting with them?

_____

What are some ways I might increase connection?

_____

Ideas, Information, and Intellect:

Do I learn new things often?

_____

Am I interested in new ideas and perspectives?

_____

Am I getting the most out of my brain power?

_____

What are some ways I might increase connection?

Organizations, Clubs, and Institutions:

Am I a member of any organizations?

Do I contribute to its growth and welfare?

What are some ways I might increase connection?

Spirituality and Personal Growth:

Do I have a spiritual practice?

Do I make time to read spiritual, uplifting books or listen to CDs or podcasts?

Do I continue to seek meaning and truth in whatever way resonates with me?

What are some ways I might increase connection?

My Relationship to Myself:

Do I meditate, have quiet time alone, know what matters most to me, and live according to it?

Am I comfortable being who I am?

What are some ways I might increase connection?

NOTES

Introduction

1. For the table, see http://www.forbes.com/sites/
johnkotter/2011/02/10/does-corporate-culture-drive-financial-
performance/.

Chapter 1

1. PricewaterhouseCoopers, "15th Annual Global CEO Survey 2012,"
available at http://www.pwc.com/gx/en/ceo-survey/pdf/15th-global-
pwc-ceo-survey.pdf.
2. Gallup, "Majority of American Workers Not Engaged in Their Jobs,"
October 2011, available at http://www.gallup.com/poll/150383/
majority-american-workers-not-engaged-jobs.aspx.

Chapter 2

1. Carl Buchheit has been a wonderful teacher to me. Find out more
about his transformative Neuro-Linguistic Programming (NLP)
techniques at http://nlpmarin.com/.
2. Brené Brown, *Daring Greatly: How the Courage to Be Vulnerable
Transforms the Way We Live, Love, Parent, and Lead* (Gotham, 2012),
16.
3. Carol Dweck, *Mindset: The New Psychology of Success* (Random House,
2006), 7.
4. Daniel J. Siegel and Tina Payne Bryson, *The Whole-Brain Child: 12
Revolutionary Strategies to Nurture Your Child's Developing Mind,
Survive Everyday Parenting Struggles, and Help Your Family Thrive*
(Delacorte Press, 2011), 62–63. See also Dr. Siegel's phenomenal
books *Mindsight: The New Science of Personal Transformation* (Bantam,
2010) and *Parenting from the Inside Out* (with Mary Hartzell; Tarcher,
2004).

Chapter 3

1. In his book *The Pause Principle: Step Back to Lean Forward* (Berrett-Koehler, 2012), Kevin Cashman tells the story of an executive who lost her voice for sixty-plus days—and had a revelation about the power of listening. As her silence unleashed her teams' natural creativity and expressiveness, she realized the best thing she could do was to listen, empower, and get out of the way. See the excerpt at http://www.fastcompany.com/3001537/how-ask-and-listen-you-mean-it?

Chapter 4

1. "Gnomes," *South Park*, South Park Studios, original air date December 18, 1998, http://www.southparkstudios.com/full-episodes/s02e17-gnomes.
2. Peter Senge, *The Fifth Discipline* (Currency/Doubleday, 1990).

Chapter 6

1. Thanks to Raz Ingrasci, founder of the Hoffman Institute (http://www.hoffmaninstitute.org/), for these statistics on the power of the emotional brain. As he puts it, "What's being learned is that theemotional brain makes decisions and our intellect is the mouthpiece. Ninety percent of the inputs to our intellect come from the emotional brain. We in the Western world think we're so logical and rational, but in fact we're not. Once we understand that, we can stop trying to change the emotions through the intellect. To use an illustration from the PBS special [*This Emotional Life*], the pathways in the brain from the emotions to the intellect are like a six-lane superhighway going in one direction. But the pathways back from the intellect to the emotions are like footpaths through the mountains." To learn more about the science behind our emotional brain, see the following resources: Harvard professor Shawn Achor's TEDxBloomington presentation, "The Happiness Advantage: Linking Positive Brains to Performance," at http://www.youtube.com/watch?v=GXy__kBVq1M; and PBS's three-part television series *This Emotional Life*, originally aired in January 2010, available at http://www.pbs.org/thisemotionallife/.
2. Chip Conley, "The Chief Emotions Officer," *Huffington Post*, April 27, 2011, http://www.huffingtonpost.com/chip-conley/the-chief-emotions-office_b_849315.html. Also see his books *Emotional Equations: Simple Truths for Creating Happiness + Success* (Free Press, 2012) and *Peak: How Great Companies Get Their Mojo from Maslow* (Jossey-Bass, 2007).
3. You can view this ad at http://www.youtube.com/watch?v=n6XZ-0ns2yA.

4. Thanks to Milton Erickson, Werner Erhard, Bryan Franklin, and the Hoffman Institute for teaching me about the power of stances.

Chapter 7

1. Rodger Bailey's work in Neuro-Linguistic Programming (NLP), particularly his Language and Behavior (LAB) Profile, is the foundation of Shelle Rose Charvet's *Words That Change Minds*.
2. Shelle Rose Charvet, *Words That Change Minds*, 2nd ed. (Kendall Hunt, 2010).

Chapter 8

1. Stephen Karpman, "Fairy Tales and Script Drama Analysis," *Transactional Analysis Bulletin* 7, no. 26 (1968): 39–43. For more on Dr. Stephen Karpman's work, see http://www.karpmandramatriangle. com/index.html.
2. David Emerald, *The Power of TED* (Polaris, 2009). See also his website, www.thepowerofted.com.

Chapter 9

1. Gregory Bateson, *Steps to an Ecology of Mind* (University of Chicago Press, 2000).
2. Phone conversation between the author and Dr. Harold Rankin, 2012.
3. John Heilpern, "When We Were 56," *Vanity Fair*, June 2012, http:// www.vanityfair.com/hollywood/2012/06/michael-apted-documentary-up-series.

Chapter 10

1. Motivation and understanding the dynamics of habits are a constant thread in Dr. Rankin's work. Two good examples of where that is articulated specifically through personal success stories are his books *Inspired to Lose* and *The TOPS Way to Weight Loss: Beyond Exercise and Calories*.

Chapter 11

1. http://blog.netflix.com/2011/09/explanation-and-some-reflections.html.

Chapter 12

1. This is a topic for another whole book, but in the meantime, see Vala Afshar and Brad Martin's book, *The Pursuit of Social Business Excellence: How to Compete, Win, and Expand Through Collaboration* (Charles Pinot, 2012).

Chapter 14

1. PricewaterhouseCoopers, "15th Annual Global CEO Survey 2012," available at http://www.pwc.com/gx/en/ceo-survey/pdf/15th-global-pwc-ceo-survey.pdf.
2. Gallup, "Majority of American Workers Not Engaged in Their Jobs," October 2011, available at http://www.gallup.com/poll/150383/majority-american-workers-not-engaged-jobs.aspx.
3. Keith Sawyer, a psychologist at Washington University, has summarized the science as follows: "Decades of research have consistently shown that brainstorming groups think of far fewer ideas than the same number of people who work alone and later pool their ideas." Read more at http://www.newyorker.com/reporting/2012/01/30/120130fa_fact_lehrer#ixzz27ydSI0aM.

Appendix

1. To take our assessment, go to www.ChristineComaford.com/lead.

INDEX